F*CK
ROCK BOTTOM

Rewrite Your Story and Rebuild Your Life
By Gaurav 'G' Patel

DEDICATION

To my father and mother, who gave me life and taught me the values of hard work, resilience, and humility. Without your love and sacrifices, none of this would have been possible.

And to my wife, Julie, my North Compass and unwavering partner, whose love, strength, and constant support have been my guardrails on this extraordinary journey. To my children, whose laughter and light remind me every day of what truly matters.

EPIGRAPH

"The darkest moments are the ones that teach you to shine the brightest."

— Anonymous

TABLE OF CONTENT

ACKNOWLEDGMENT

This book is not merely the account of my journey—it is a testament to the collective influence, inspiration, and support of the extraordinary people who have shaped my life and this story. It would not exist without the community that has surrounded me, lifted me, and taught me what it means to persevere.

To my parents, your wisdom and sacrifices are the bedrock upon which my entire life has been built. You taught me the value of grit, the importance of integrity, and the power of humility. These lessons have been my guiding compass, and I am forever indebted to you.

To my wife Julie, your strength, grace, and unwavering belief in me have been my greatest anchor through the highs and lows. Thank you for being the steadfast partner who reminds me daily of what truly matters.

To my children, your joy and light are constant reminders that life's greatest gifts come from connection, wonder, and love. You inspire me to be better every single day.

To the mentors, teachers, and leaders who challenged my perspective, fueled my growth, and dared me to dream bigger: your impact echoes through every word in this book. To my friends, who stood beside me in moments of both triumph and despair, your loyalty and presence have been my strongest shield and my greatest comfort.

To my partners and teams at CityPlat, your shared vision, camaraderie, and relentless drive have been the spark behind so many incredible moments. Together, we have built something extraordinary, and I am grateful for the journey we continue to forge.

To Erich Schlenker and Rick Martinez, your extraordinary ability to extract, refine, and bring to life the core essence of this book has been nothing short of transformative. Your dedication to this project, coupled with your unwavering patience and insight, has elevated this story into something I am profoundly proud to share with the world.

And to my community—both near and far, familiar and unfamiliar— thank you. Your encouragement, your belief, and even your silent presence have been pivotal in fueling my determination.

Finally, to you, the reader: this book was written with the hope that it inspires you to embrace your own journey, no matter how challenging or uncertain. Writing this has been one of the most humbling and enlightening experiences of my life, and I am profoundly grateful for the opportunity to share it with you.

Thank you all for being part of this incredible journey.

**Rock bottom isn't the end—it's your restart.
Reclaim, Rebuild, and Recalibrate your story.**

INTRODUCTION

When Rock Bottom Becomes Your Launchpad

I didn't write this book because I've always had it figured out. I didn't write it because I'm a guru with all the answers or some motivational speaker with a foolproof formula for success. I wrote it because I've been compelled to share my story—a story that has resonated with those who have urged me time and again to put it into words. This book comes from a place of humility and a desire to connect, inspire, and guide others through the struggles I know all too well. I wrote it because I've been there. I've felt lost, overwhelmed, and uncertain about the future, wondering if I could ever find a way forward.

Honestly, I never aspired to be an author—just like I never aspired to be a restaurateur or even an entrepreneur. Life, in its unpredictable ways, has a knack for showing us paths we never imagined walking. And so, here I am, putting my story into words because the lessons I've learned along the way feel too valuable to keep to myself. Time and again, friends, colleagues, and even strangers have told me, "You should share your story." They've said it's powerful, that it could help others. For years, I brushed it off, doubting myself, wondering if I had anything worth saying—the classic struggle with imposter syndrome.

But here's the truth: I've learned through the messiness of life that sharing our experiences—the good, the bad, and the rock bottom—has the power to connect, to heal, and to inspire. This book is my attempt to do just that. It's not perfect, and neither am I, but it's the best I can give.

I've been at the edge, staring into the void, wondering if life was even worth it anymore. I've felt the crushing weight of what the world calls failure—professional, personal, and everything in between. I've sat in silence as life seemed to move on without me, leaving me in the wreckage of my decisions.

You'll hear a lot about that night in the tub—the night when the scissors on the edge felt like the only way out. That moment, though deeply personal, speaks to a universal struggle: the crushing weight of feeling like you've hit an unmovable wall. But this book isn't just about that moment. It's about everything that led me there: the triumphs that turned to ash, the successes that felt hollow, the fights, the silence, and the unbearable sense of emptiness when everything I thought I was crumbled to the ground.

More importantly, though, this book is about what came next. It's about the climb—the grueling, ugly, soul-shaking work of rebuilding a life from scratch. It's about resilience, the kind that kicks in when you're at your weakest, when you think you're done, and when you're ready to throw in the towel. And it's about recalibrating—not just clawing your way back to where you were but creating a new, truer, better version of yourself in the process. For me, that meant reconnecting with my family, starting therapy, and eventually finding new purpose in mentoring others and rebuilding my career in ways I never imagined possible.

This is my story, but it's also yours. It's for anyone who's ever felt like the weight of the world is too much to carry. It's for anyone who's ever sat in silence, staring at the rubble of their life and wondering, *What the fuck do I do now?*

Here's the thing: hitting rock bottom doesn't mean the end. It means you've been handed a clean slate—a brutal, painful, and raw opportunity to start over. This book is about turning that place of despair into a launchpad for your greatest comeback.

Together, we'll explore the hard truths about what I now call catalysts—the pivotal moments that force us to face ourselves. For me, one of those catalysts was the night I sat in that tub, overwhelmed and broken, realizing something had to change. They aren't the end; they're the turning points. Along the way, I'll share

v

the steps that helped me crawl out of the darkness and recalibrate my life—not to what it was before but to something greater.

This journey isn't easy. It's raw. It's messy. It's uncomfortable. But if you're ready to stop living for what the world expects of you and start living for what you truly deserve, then this book is for you. Whether you're grappling with a career setback, a personal loss, or the overwhelming feeling of being stuck, the lessons in this book are meant to resonate with anyone ready to rewrite their story.

So let's begin.

Because from the ashes of despair, we can rise stronger. From the depths of chaos, we can create something extraordinary. And from this moment, we can take the first step toward becoming the person we were always meant to be.

CHAPTER 1: THE TUB

The scissors sat there, gleaming on the edge of the tub—a silent witness to the chaos storming through my head. My face hovered just above the water's surface, each shaky breath sending ripples through the stillness. The faint hum of the vanity light overhead flickered, casting a dull glow across the room. My heart thudded in my ears, drowning out everything else.

How the fuck did it spiral out of control so fast?

The mounting failures, the constant pressure to perform, and the relentless demands I placed on myself had all snowballed. Each setback chipped away at my confidence, and I found myself slipping further, unable to regain control. It felt like the world was closing in, faster than I could manage, until there was nothing left to hold onto.

In movies, when one jet engine flames out, there's hope. You stabilize, fight for control, and limp to a runway. But when the second engine flames out and the fuel gauge is empty, the earth doesn't give you time to react. It rushes toward you, faster than any Hollywood script could ever capture.

And there it was again, that same thought, like a jackhammer to the skull:

How did it get out of control so fast?

For a while, I convinced myself I could pull it off. I could stabilize, fix it, land this thing. I was trained for this. Hell, I was born for this. I was the pilot—the guy who navigates storms and always came out victorious. But no one warns you about the weight of failure.

Nobody tells you how heavy it is.

1

It's not just emotional weight—the shame, the guilt, the regret—but a physical and mental heaviness that makes every movement feel like wading through quicksand. It's the kind of weight that drags you down, refusing to let you breathe, refusing to let you rise.

And then, without warning, it all crashes.

There's no time to brace. No heroic maneuver. Just impact.

The problem was, there was no jet. The jet was my life. And now, here I was, staring at those scissors like they were the last tool I'd ever need.

I was crying so hard I couldn't see straight. My vision blurred as tears streamed down my face, mixing with the sting of salt and the ache that pulsed in my chest. My head throbbed, and my throat burned with every ragged breath, as if my body itself was revolting against the weight of my emotions. My body trembled, chest heaving as sobs racked through me.

I was ready.

The bathroom light flickered weakly, its reflection shimmering on the water like a dying ember. The soft sloshing of the tub echoed louder than it should have, like the universe amplifying every thought.

"Man, I hope the water isn't spilling onto the floor," I thought. Even at rock bottom, I wanted to keep the mess contained. That's me, I guess—always trying to control the chaos, even as I drowned in it.

I closed my eyes and let out a trembling breath. I wasn't sure where the tremble came from—fear? Exhaustion? Or maybe relief. Relief that I wouldn't have to fight anymore.

The Fucking Article

Months earlier, *The Triangle Business Journal* had blown my life wide open:

2

"Prominent Raleigh Restaurateur Files for Chapter 11 Bankruptcy."

The meeting had started fine. The Social House Vodka boardroom had that polished, high-stakes vibe—glass walls, sleek leather chairs, and a skyline view that screamed success. Investors leaned in as I spoke, nodding at every point. My partner was flipping through slides: sales trajectories, expansion plans, projections that painted a rosy picture of the future.

We were pitching $4 million in funding to scale the business.

And then my partner's phone buzzed.

I saw the way his jaw clenched, his fingers pausing over the presentation remote. My phone buzzed next, and everything froze.

The article was live. The timing couldn't have been worse. This wasn't supposed to happen until next week, after we closed the deal. But now the news was everywhere.

"Prominent Raleigh Restaurateur Files for Chapter 11 Bankruptcy."

My partner leaned in. "The article's live," he said under his breath. "They know everything."

The weight hit me like a freight train. My head swam. The air in the room seemed to shift, like the oxygen had been sucked out. How do you pivot from that? How do you tell a room full of people who've trusted you with their money that your financial life just went up in flames?

I cleared my throat. My voice felt distant, like it belonged to someone else.

"Before we continue, I need to share some news," I began. The words were rehearsed, but they felt hollow.

"The *Triangle Business Journal* just published a story about me. It details my personal bankruptcy filing. I want to be transparent with you all about what's happening."

The room was silent. Some investors leaned forward, their brows furrowed. Others leaned back, crossing their arms.

"This filing doesn't affect Social House," I continued, forcing my voice to stay steady. "The distillery is insulated. The challenges I've faced are tied to my other ventures. I believe in what we're building here, and I'm committed to seeing it succeed."

It sounded convincing. But deep down, I knew the truth: the first domino had fallen.

The article didn't stop at the headline. The reporter dug deep. All judgments, failed ventures. Frozen accounts. They even listed the value of my assets, my personal jewelry, and, absurdly, my fucking dog and his age.

Seeing my entire life dissected and laid bare for public consumption felt like being stripped of all dignity. Professionally, it was catastrophic—investors and partners started questioning everything. Personally, it was soul-crushing, a magnifying glass placed over every mistake, every misstep. It wasn't just a news story; it was a blow that left me reeling, wondering if there was any way back from this.

My dog, really?

Rock Bottom

By the time I climbed into the tub that night, the months of failure had worn me down. I was drunk, high, and hollow. Julie and I had fought earlier that evening—words exchanged that cut deep, though they didn't matter now. Nothing mattered.

The scissors sat there, waiting.

Pick me up, G.

Stop being a coward, G.

I grabbed them, the cold steel pressing into my palm. My chest felt like it was being crushed under a boulder, every breath harder than the last.

"Please," I whispered, tears streaming down my face and mingling with the bathwater. *"Please, just give me a reason to keep going."*

The Voice That Saved Me

*"Guvu!"

Her voice shattered the silence like a thunderclap.*

"Guvu! Open this door right now!"

The scissors slipped from my hand, clattering loudly against the tub. My body froze.

"Beta, please!" she cried, her voice trembling.

My hand moved before my mind could catch up. I unlocked the door.

And there she was, my mother. Small but fierce, her presence filled the room like a lifeline. Her eyes, glistening with tears, locked onto mine. She didn't yell. She didn't demand an explanation. She just stepped forward and wrapped her arms around me.

"You're going to be okay," she whispered, her voice steady even as her tears fell onto my shoulder. *"We'll get through this. I promise."*

And for the first time in months, I believed her.

A Thread of Hope Emerges

Rock bottom doesn't come with fireworks or dramatic music. It sneaks in quietly. It's the flicker of a dying lightbulb. The cold edge of scissors in your hand. The sound of water rippling in a bathtub.

That night wasn't redemption. It wasn't the moment my life turned around.

But it was a thread—a fragile, invisible thread that reminded me I wasn't completely alone. And that thread became the starting point of something greater. It was the first step toward resilience, a moment that forced me to confront the darkness and choose to fight back.

Sometimes, all it takes is one thread. One voice. One moment to remind you that transformation begins in the smallest, quietest ways.

And that's exactly what I held onto.

CHAPTER 2: UNSHAKABLE FOUNDATION

The door flung open, and the blinding midday sun streamed in as my mother cupped her hands around her mouth and called my name, her voice cutting through the familiar hum of the village.

"Guvu! Come home!"

Her voice rang out, cutting through the buzz of the midday heat and the distant murmur of village life. It carried an urgency that tugged at my chest—a mixture of impatience, authority, and the kind of love only a mother's call could hold.

That voice—it was always equal parts authority and love. And in our tiny village of Zervavra, it echoed like a bell, carrying a weight only mothers can wield.

My gut told me I was in trouble. I mean, whenever my name was yelled like that, it usually meant one thing: a reckoning. Whether it was stealing mangos, wandering too far into the fields, or being somewhere I wasn't supposed to be, my adventures usually earned me a swift and memorable consequence.

But this time, it wasn't about trouble. It was yogurt.

"Come inside and have some yogurt!" she shouted again, her tone shifting to the impatient melody of someone who knew I'd be poking at mud with a stick until sunset if left alone.

That's the thing about my mom—she never let the chaos I created cloud the tenderness she offered. And in Zervavra, yogurt wasn't just a snack; it was a treat. Homemade from scratch, fermented with care and consistency. My mother would start the process by boiling fresh milk, letting it cool just enough before adding a dollop of culture saved from the last batch. She'd cover it with a cloth and let it sit in a warm corner, where time and patience would transform it into the creamy, tangy yogurt that was a staple of our meals. It wasn't just food; it was a ritual, one passed down through generations, binding us to our heritage and the rhythms of village life. There was no corner store, no prepackaged tubs, no rows of endless choices. You made do with what you had, and when something was made, it was savored.

A Childhood Rooted in Simplicity

Zervavra, Gujarat. A village of barely 150 people. Cow-dung brick homes, ancient banyan trees, and fields stretching endlessly into the horizon. Mornings began with the melodic cooing of doves and the distant moo of cattle being herded. By midday, the air would hum with the steady buzz of cicadas, punctuated by the occasional shout of children playing tag in the fields. Evenings brought the scent of wood smoke mingling with the earthy aroma of damp soil as the village prepared for nightfall.

Running water? No.

Electricity? Sometimes, if we were lucky.

But it didn't matter. This was home.

My great-grandfather's house stood just a stone's throw from the village temple, a spire reaching toward the heavens. The temple wasn't just a place of worship; it was the heartbeat of the village. Weddings, celebrations, and festivals always began and ended there. It was where lessons in discipline, gratitude, and interconnectedness were silently taught, simply by being part of the community.

I didn't know what I didn't have, and I didn't care. Ignorance truly was bliss.

A Little Terror

Looking back, I was a wild child. Rambunctious, stubborn, and always on the move. I pushed boundaries—not because I wanted to rebel but because I was curious. What was beyond the temple? Beyond the banyan tree? Beyond the fields?

Trouble wasn't my goal, but it was often the byproduct of my adventures. Like the time I built a raft out of bamboo poles and tried to float it down the irrigation canal, only to capsize and come home drenched, dragging the soggy remains behind me. Or when I dared my friends to climb the tallest banyan tree, only to realize halfway up that we had no plan to get back down. Each escapade earned me a mix of scolding and laughter, but they fed my endless curiosity and boundless energy. Like the time I climbed a tree to steal mangos from someone else's crop. I still remember the sting of my mother's switch across my legs when she found out. She wasn't angry because I'd taken something; she was angry because I hadn't thought about the work that went into growing it.

"Respect the hands that labor," she'd say.

And respect was a lesson that took root early. Whether it was for the farmer tending the fields or the woman cooking chapatis over an open flame, Zervavra taught me to see value in effort.

The Lesson of the Yogurt

When I sprinted home that day, panting and dusty, my mother stood in the doorway with her arms crossed, half-exasperated and half-amused. The bowl of yogurt sat on the wooden table behind her, its creamy surface smooth and inviting.

"Sit," she said, pointing to the chair.

As I took my first bite, the tangy sweetness hit my tongue, and for a moment, everything stopped. It wasn't just food—it was a connection. A reminder that no matter how far I wandered, no matter what trouble I found, there was always something to ground me.

Looking back now, that yogurt wasn't just a treat. It was an anchor. It symbolized a home, a family, and a village that, while small, gave me everything I needed to grow strong roots.

The Foundations of Resilience

Zervavra taught me that life is built on the simplest things:

- **Hard work,** because nothing comes easy. I remember the harvest season vividly, when the entire village came together to gather crops. The sun would beat down relentlessly, and my small hands would ache from hours of pulling weeds or carrying bundles of grain. Yet, no one complained. The satisfaction of seeing a full cart of fresh produce was its own reward, a reminder that effort and perseverance always bore fruit—literally and figuratively.
- **Community,** because no one succeeds alone. When one family struggled, the entire village stepped in to help. I remember when heavy rains threatened to wash away the crops, and neighbors worked shoulder to shoulder to dig trenches and redirect the water. That unity wasn't just practical; it was life-saving.
- **Gratitude,** because even the smallest things—like a bowl of yogurt—carry infinite value. I learned to be thankful for what we had, no matter how modest, and to recognize that abundance comes in many forms.

But resilience isn't just about enduring; it's about adapting and growing. Like the banyan tree in the village square, whose roots grew deep and spread wide, resilience is the strength to weather storms and still reach for the light.

I've carried those lessons with me far beyond Zervavra, through the trials and failures of my adult life. Resilience taught me to keep moving, even when the road ahead seemed impossible. It reminded me that every setback is temporary, and that the foundations built on hard work, community, and gratitude are unshakable.

-

Takeaway: Build Your Own Foundation

As you navigate your journey, remember this: success isn't just about reaching the top. It's about the roots you plant and the foundation you stand on. Here are three steps to build your own unshakable foundation:

- **Reconnect with Your Core Values**
  What principles guide your decisions? Family? Integrity? Hard work? Write them down, and commit to living by them.
- **Create Rituals That Ground You**
  Whether it's a daily walk, a quiet moment of reflection, or a bowl of yogurt, find small practices that keep you connected to what matters most.
- **Lean on Your Community**
  Nobody succeeds alone, succeeding alone is an oxymoron. Surround yourself with people who uplift and challenge you, and don't be afraid to lean on them when the road gets tough.

Your foundation doesn't have to be perfect. It just has to be strong enough to hold you when the winds of life threaten to knock you down.

CHAPTER 3: MY NEW WORLD

Arriving in Morehead City, North Carolina, felt like stepping into another universe. Everything was alien—the streets, lined with unfamiliar architecture and glowing traffic lights, the people, whose accents sounded musical yet incomprehensible to my ears, the smells, a mix of salty ocean air and fresh asphalt. Even the sky seemed different, a vast expanse of blue that stretched endlessly, unbroken by the towering banyan trees I had known all my life. The air carried a salty tang from the nearby ocean, a scent so foreign it might as well have been from another planet. I was ten years old, clutching a small bag of belongings, my entire world uprooted from Zervavra and planted in a place that seemed impossibly vast.

I didn't speak a word of English.

The House of Wonders

The 20-room hotel my uncle owned became our first home in America. Our family of four was given a single motel room to share. It was modest, with just enough space for a bed, a small dresser, and our few belongings tucked neatly into one corner. The constant buzz of the front desk phone, the muffled chatter of guests, and the occasional clang of vending machines created an entirely new soundtrack for our lives.

Behind the check-in desk, my uncle's family lived in a small set of quarters. This space quickly became the heart of our new reality. The kitchen, located there, was where my extended family—14 of us in total—would gather for meals. At dinner, we crowded into the living room behind the front desk, plates balanced on laps, sharing stories and laughter. It was cramped and chaotic, but it was also comforting.

The contrasts between this new life and our old one in India couldn't have been starker. Back home, our house had sturdy concrete walls reinforced with clay and cow dung bricks, built to endure the monsoons. Here, the walls were smooth and sterile, without the earthy warmth I'd grown up with. Home-cooked meals, prepared on open flames and seasoned with care, were replaced by dishes hurriedly assembled in a small kitchen bustling with overlapping voices. While I marveled at the conveniences of running water and electric light, my heart ached for the familiar chaos and grounded simplicity of Zervavra.

Yet, even in this unfamiliar world, family was our constant. The living room dinners and shared stories became our anchor, reminding us that home wasn't just a place—it was the people who filled it with love and resilience.

But it wasn't home.

Reality of the American Dream

When we arrived in Morehead City, my parents didn't waste a single moment. Just days after stepping off the plane, they began working at my uncle's 20-room motel. It wasn't glamorous, but it was an opportunity—one they embraced with grit and determination. They started their days before dawn, cleaning rooms, scrubbing toilets, and folding endless piles of sheets. They worked tirelessly, their faces etched with exhaustion, but they never complained.

The motel became more than just their workplace; it was where we all lived and built our lives together. Meals were shared in the living quarters behind the front desk, where the kitchen buzzed with activity. Every evening, we gathered as a family—14 of us crammed into the small living room—to share food, laughter, and stories. Despite the chaos, it was these moments that reminded us of the bonds that held us together.

"Gaurav," my father would say, his voice steady but firm. "In America, you can be anything. You just have to work for it."

I nodded, not fully understanding the weight of his words. How could I? I was ten, overwhelmed by the strangeness of it all. But watching them work, I began to grasp the sacrifices they were making, and the unwavering belief they had in this new chapter for our family.

School - My Battlefield

The first day of school began with a sense of confusion and wonder. My cousins and I walked from the motel's living quarters to the edge of the road. I remember standing there, staring at the pavement, and asking my cousin Mital,

"Why are we just standing here?"

Before he could answer, a big yellow bus rolled to a stop in front of us. It was the first time I'd ever seen a school bus. I was astonished.

The bus ride itself was quiet. Mital, who had been born in the U.S., stayed by my side, but even he seemed unsure of how to navigate this new dynamic. When we arrived at the school, I was ushered into a classroom that felt overwhelmingly bright and noisy. My teacher, Miss Monroe, smiled warmly, but the other kids weren't so kind.

"Where are you from?" one boy asked loudly, his freckled face scrunched in mock curiosity. "Do you even speak English?"

The laughter stung more than I expected. I didn't understand the words, but their tone was universal. It said: You don't belong here.

That moment planted a seed of determination in me. I didn't want to feel that sting again. The isolation, the taunts, the invisible barrier between me and my peers—they became fuel. I resolved to prove, not just to them but to myself, that I could overcome this. It wasn't just about learning a new language; it was about transforming how I saw myself in this unfamiliar world. Every cruel laugh became a reason to try harder, every misunderstanding a push to adapt faster.

I sat at the back of the classroom, trying to make myself invisible. The lessons were incomprehensible, the teacher's words a jumble of unfamiliar sounds. My mind wandered back to Zervavra, to the temple spire that reached for the heavens, to the laughter of my friends as we chased each other through the fields.

Ignorance was bliss, they say. But in that moment, ignorance was the cage.

Language of Survival

Determined not to let the taunts define me, I made a plan. I would learn English, no matter how hard it was. My first teachers? Cartoons. I sat for hours in front of the TV, watching Teenage Mutant Ninja Turtles, absorbing words and phrases like a sponge. Leo, Ralph, Donnie, and Mikey became my first American friends, teaching me not just the language but the attitude I needed to survive.

But the most profound help came from Miss Monroe. Recognizing how much I was struggling, she would sit me outside the classroom with an old television and let me watch Sesame Street. Those cheerful puppets, with their simple songs and playful interactions, became my lifeline. I repeated letters with Big Bird and counted along with the Count. Day by day, I started learning my ABCs, piecing together the building blocks of a new language.

Every small victory felt monumental. The first time I understood a full sentence, the first joke I told that landed with laughter, the first time I greeted a classmate without hesitation—each moment chipped away at the barriers between me and this new world. Slowly but surely, those victories built my confidence. I realized that the effort I put in, no matter how daunting, always led to progress. That understanding became my anchor, helping me approach every challenge with the belief that I could overcome it.

I mimicked everything—the way they spoke, the way they moved, even their jokes. I practiced words under my breath until they stopped feeling foreign in my mouth. Slowly, I began to pick up the rhythm of the language, the way sentences flowed, the way words connected.

But it wasn't just about learning English. It was about fitting in.

Becoming "G"

One of the first changes I made was my name. My full name— Gauravkumar Mahendrakumar Patel—consisted of 29 letters, a puzzle for anyone trying to read it. Every time a teacher or classmate attempted, it would twist and turn, becoming unrecognizable.

At first, I shortened it to Gaurav Mahendra Patel, simplifying things slightly. But even that wasn't enough when I started taking standardized tests. I remember filling out Scantron forms with my impossibly long name, running out of space and hoping the machine wouldn't reject it. Those moments were both frustrating and absurd, and I often joked that my name alone could cost me points on a test.

As time passed, I shed more and more of my name. First, Kumar disappeared, then Gaurav became just "G." It wasn't just a practical choice—it was an evolution. Becoming "G" was more than a linguistic shortcut; it was survival, adaptation, and a touch of humor all rolled into one. It was about blending in, but also about finding a version of myself that worked in this new world.

And yet, I never saw it as losing my identity. Instead, it was a bridge—a way to connect my roots to my present. I kept the pride of my full name alive in my heart, but "G" allowed me to navigate a world that had no idea how to pronounce it. It became my symbol of adaptability and resilience, one letter that carried the weight of an entire journey.

Becoming "G" was more than just a linguistic shortcut; it was a transformation. I wanted to be a chameleon, someone who could move seamlessly between worlds, adapting to any environment. I wanted to belong—not just to the Indian community, but to the broader world I saw around me.

This desire to fit in wasn't just about survival. It was about opportunity. I started to realize that the more I blended in, the more doors might open. And so, I worked at it relentlessly.

Culture Shock and Adaptability

Morehead City wasn't a sprawling metropolis but rather a quaint beach town with a close-knit, laid-back vibe. The streets were lined with small local shops, the air carried a constant salty breeze, and retirees leisurely strolled along the waterfront. It felt like a world away from the vast farmlands and a small community life of Zervavra.

In Zervavra, community was everything. People relied on each other, shared what little they had, and came together in times of need. In Morehead City, everything felt individualistic. People seemed tucked away in their homes, focused on their own routines. That stark contrast left me feeling unmoored, navigating a culture that was foreign and isolating.

One pivotal moment came during my time at school, a day I'd rather forget but one that shaped me deeply. I passed a note in my science class—a dumb, juvenile prank that somehow spiraled out of control. The note - "*schools gonna blow after lunch*" caused a misunderstanding, and the school evacuated under the impression of a bomb threat. I was mortified as the principal sternly explained the seriousness of what I'd done. My father was called to the school, and his face when he arrived—a mix of disappointment and worry—is something I'll never forget.

"You were supposed to make the most of this opportunity," he said later that night. "Not waste it."

The weight of those words settled heavily on me. I realized in that moment that the sacrifices my parents had made to bring us to America weren't just about giving me a better life; they were about trust and responsibility. From that day on, I understood that adaptation wasn't just about survival. It was about making something meaningful out of every opportunity, no matter how challenging it seemed.

I began to embrace change, learning to adapt to my new surroundings while holding onto the values that had shaped me. It wasn't about letting go of who I was but finding ways to integrate my roots into this new world. Adaptation became my greatest strength, a skill that allowed me to navigate complexities and build a bridge between my past and present. Through every challenge, I learned to thrive, understanding that growth was a choice I had to make daily.

-

The Takeaway: Adaptation is a Superpower

Adapting to a new world isn't about changing who you are. It's about finding the balance between staying true to your roots and embracing the new. I remember one instance when my classmates invited me to join their lunchtime basketball games. I was hesitant at first—basketball was as foreign to me as their language. But I decided to try, and though I stumbled through the first few games, I quickly realized how much I enjoyed it. Soon, I was teaching them a game from India called kabaddi, and to my surprise, they loved it. Those moments taught me that adaptation could be a two-way street, blending cultures to create connections and mutual respect.

Here's what I learned:

- **Language Is Power**
  Learning the language of your environment—whether it's a literal language or the unspoken rules of a new culture—is the first step to integration.
- **Reinvent Without Losing Yourself**
  Adapting doesn't mean abandoning who you are. It means building bridges between your past and your present.
- **Resilience Is Built, Not Born**
  Each challenge, each failure, each misstep is an opportunity to grow stronger. Adaptation isn't a one-time thing; it's a lifelong process.
- **Community Matters**
  Surround yourself with people who believe in you, who guide you, and who remind you of what's possible.

My life wasn't just about surviving—it was about learning to thrive, to embrace change, and to see every new challenge as a chance to build something better. It was the beginning of understanding that adaptation isn't a compromise; it's a strength.

CHAPTER 4: RELEARNING THE RULES

Moving back to North Carolina after our stint in Mississippi felt like coming home, but not entirely. Home in Jackson, Mississippi had been different—filled with its own struggles, lessons, and moments of growth. Returning to North Carolina brought a mix of familiarity and unease. We weren't going back to the exact comfort of what we had left, but instead stepping into a new chapter that required its own set of adjustments. Havelock wasn't just another place; it was the canvas on which I'd start to redefine my sense of belonging and identity. We weren't returning to Morehead City; instead, we settled in Havelock. By then, I'd grown used to starting over, but it didn't make the process any easier. Each new beginning brought its own challenges, its own set of rules to relearn.

Havelock was different, yet the essence of what I'd learned from Morehead City and Jackson stayed with me: adapt, absorb, and find your place. But Havelock wasn't about fitting in—it became the place where I started figuring out how to stand out.

Havelock was quieter than Jackson, a small military town where everyone seemed to know everyone else. My family moved into a modest home that reflected the progress my parents had made since arriving in the United States. The trailer park days were behind us, but the hustle never stopped.

By this point, I was in middle school, and my English was far better. I no longer stumbled over words or phrases, but my accent—or lack thereof—still surprised people. "You sound so American," some kids would say, a backhanded compliment that reminded me I was still different.

But here's the thing: by then, I didn't care about fitting in. Havelock became my proving ground, the place where I stopped trying to hide my differences and started embracing them. One moment that marked this shift was when I joined the debate club. Initially, I felt out of place—my accent still stood out, and I worried about being judged. But as I spoke up more, I realized my unique perspective often brought something valuable to the conversation. Another defining moment was during a community event where I volunteered to help organize a fundraiser. My ideas, rooted in a blend of my upbringing and new experiences, were well-received, and for the first time, I felt pride in what set me apart. These moments taught me that my differences weren't obstacles; they were assets that allowed me to contribute in ways others couldn't.

Rewriting the Rules

It was in Havelock that I discovered the thrill of entrepreneurship. My parents' relentless work ethic had rubbed off on me, but I wanted something that was mine. My first venture? Flipping candy bars.

I'd buy bulk packs of chocolate from the store and sell them to my classmates at a markup. It wasn't revolutionary, but it was a taste of independence. I still remember one memorable sale—a classmate who initially scoffed at my markup but later returned, craving the chocolate bar I had on hand. "Fine, take my money," he said grudgingly, and I realized then how much power there was in timing and understanding demand. That little win taught me that creating value wasn't just about the product—it was about being at the right place at the right time with the right solution. I learned how to negotiate, how to read people, and, most importantly, how to create value. My little candy empire wasn't about making money—it was about discovering that I had the power to create opportunities.

Looking back, it's funny how something as small as selling candy bars could teach such big lessons. It wasn't just about the hustle; *it was about the mindset.* I learned that if you could spot a need and fill it, you could thrive anywhere.

Pushing Boundaries

As I settled into Havelock, my rebellious streak began to reemerge, but in ways that reflected my curiosity and drive rather than simple defiance. One defining moment was when I decided to build my first website for a local business. It wasn't just about the technical challenge; it was about pushing past the idea that someone my age couldn't contribute meaningfully to the business world. I still remember the moment when I pitched the idea and was handed my first $2,000 check from the local Dodge dealership. That experience taught me that breaking boundaries wasn't about being reckless; it was about daring to believe I could offer value where no one expected it.

Pushing boundaries became a philosophy, a way of questioning the framework rather than merely defying it. It wasn't about rebellion for its own sake but about discovering where innovation could thrive and growth could flourish. Testing limits revealed that some rules were meant to guide, while others required reimagining. It was less about breaking and more about creating—channeling energy into reshaping the world, not disrupting it.

Those moments shaped my confidence and helped me realize that my rebellious nature could be channeled into something constructive. I wasn't just testing limits for the thrill of it—I was defining new possibilities for myself.

Turning Point

It wasn't one event or moment that changed things—it was a series of small realizations that built up over time. The drive to question the status quo became my guiding principle. I began to understand that *my rebellious nature wasn't a flaw; it was a strength*. It wasn't about disrupting for the sake of it—it was about channeling that energy into creating meaningful change and finding better ways to navigate the world around me.

One of the most profound lessons I learned during this time was that questioning the rules often led to growth. Whether it was asking why certain systems worked the way they did or experimenting with unconventional approaches, I discovered that pushing boundaries could open doors to opportunities I hadn't imagined. I also realized that *I didn't need to create chaos to make my mark*—I could carve my path with intention and purpose, challenging norms while fostering progress.

For instance, joining the debate club taught me more than just how to speak. It taught me how to think critically, challenge assumptions, and present ideas that shifted perspectives. Similarly, building my first website for a local business wasn't just about earning money. It was about proving that ability transcends age. Earning that $2,000 check showed me that taking calculated risks and embracing unconventional thinking could yield results that surprised not only others but also myself.

These experiences reinforced the idea that growth came from stepping outside comfort zones, questioning norms, and daring to believe in possibilities others couldn't see. My rebellious nature, when harnessed, became a tool for innovation and transformation— a driving force in shaping the person I was becoming.

The Bigger Picture

Havelock wasn't just another stop on our journey—it was the place where I began to understand the bigger picture. It wasn't enough to adapt or survive; I wanted to thrive. I wanted to build something that was mine, something that would last.

My parents' sacrifices weren't just about giving me a better life— they were about giving me the tools to create one. I remember watching my father work endless night shifts, his hands worn from scrubbing and cleaning, yet his resolve never wavering. One evening, he sat me down and said,

"Guvu, hard work doesn't guarantee success, but without it, you'll never even get close."

Those words stayed with me, shaping how I approached every challenge. Their relentless effort wasn't just to provide; it was to show me what perseverance looked like, planting the seeds of resilience and determination that I would carry into every aspect of my life. Every late-night shift they worked, every penny they saved, every piece of advice they gave—it all added up to a foundation that I could build on.

The Takeaway: Turning Rebellion Into Purpose

Havelock taught me that rebellion isn't inherently bad—it's all about how you channel it. Here's what I learned:

- **Question Everything**
  Rules aren't sacred. Challenge them, test them, and figure out which ones serve you and which ones hold you back.
- **Find Your Hustle**
  Whether it's selling candy bars or starting a business, find something that's yours. It's not about the money—it's about the independence and confidence it gives you.
- **Embrace Your Differences**
  Stop trying to fit in. Your differences are your strengths, the things that set you apart and make you valuable.
- **Build on Your Foundations**
  Remember where you came from, but don't let it limit you. Use it as a springboard to reach higher.

This chapter of my life wasn't perfect, but it was pivotal. It was where I learned that success isn't about following the rules—it's about rewriting them. It's about taking what you've been given and turning it into something extraordinary. And most importantly, it's about believing in yourself, even when no one else does.

CHAPTER 5: THE SPARK

Raleigh felt like a city of endless possibilities. Moving here at the age of sixteen to attend Wake Tech was a fresh start, but it came with its own set of challenges. I was juggling three jobs, struggling to make ends meet, and trying to keep up with my coursework. The weight of it all felt suffocating.

Something had to give.

Sitting in my car late one night after a long shift, I made a decision: I couldn't keep living like this. I needed to find a way to work smarter, not harder. And that's when the idea of throwing events came to me—a chance to lean into my strengths and create something on my own terms.

The idea didn't come to me all at once—it started small, almost accidentally. A few months after moving to Raleigh, I began inviting new friends over to my place. At first, it was just five of us hanging out on a weekend, sharing laughs and stories. The next weekend, that five turned into ten. Then it was twenty. Before long, my living room was packed with 30 or 40 people, all just enjoying the energy we created together.

It was during one of those nights, looking around at a room full of people who had come together because of something I started, that the spark ignited. I loved the vibe, the connection, and the sense of community. That's when I realized I could take this to the next level. What if I turned these gatherings into something bigger? What if I could create spaces where people could come together, have a great time, and escape the pressures of school and work? And what if I could make money doing it?

The concept wasn't polished, but the drive was there. I'd always been someone who thrived on bringing people together, and now I saw an opportunity to turn that knack into something meaningful.

That spark of an idea wasn't just about parties; it was the beginning of my entrepreneurial journey. I didn't know it then, but this was where it all truly began.

The First Event

The first event wasn't just a leap of faith; it was a culmination of relentless effort, small savings, and sheer determination. After the idea struck, I began knocking on doors, quite literally. I approached venues I knew weren't making much money on certain nights—small nightclubs and lounges that sat dormant during the week. With a mix of confidence and persistence, I pitched my idea: let me use their space to host an event, and we'd split the profits. After a lot of handshakes, a few rejections, and plenty of persuasion, I finally found a venue willing to take a chance on me.

I'd saved up just enough money from working three jobs to cover the upfront costs—about $500 for the venue, a DJ, and printing flyers. It wasn't much, but for me, it was everything. I plastered those flyers across the NC State, Duke, and Chapel Hill campuses, going dorm to dorm, lamp post to lamp post, selling the idea to anyone who'd listen. It was old-school marketing: face-to-face interactions, hustling in hallways, and making sure people saw my enthusiasm. There was no social media blitz, no viral campaign—just determination and a willingness to shake hands and kiss babies, as they say.

The night of the event, my nerves were on edge. What if no one showed? What if I failed? I watched the clock, second-guessing every decision. But then, as the start time approached, people began to arrive.

First a few.

Then a dozen.

And then they came in waves.

Before I knew it, the venue was packed. Over 200 people showed up that night, each paying $10 at the door. The DJ kept the energy alive, the crowd was electric, and the vibe was everything I'd hoped for and more. By the end of the night, after paying off expenses, I walked away with $1,500 in profit. For a 17-year-old college student, it felt like I'd hit the jackpot.

But it wasn't just the money. It was the realization that I'd created something from nothing—that with the right mix of hustle, charm, and risk-taking, I could make an idea come to life. That night wasn't just a party; it was proof that I could chart my own path. It was the moment I stopped dreaming and started doing, and it set the stage for everything that came next.

Building Momentum

With the success of my first event, I knew I was onto something. Over the next few months, I threw myself into the business. I learned how to negotiate better deals with venues, how to market more effectively, and how to create events that people couldn't stop talking about. I expanded my reach, partnering with other students and local businesses to bring in bigger crowds.

It wasn't easy. There were late nights, stressful negotiations, and plenty of moments when things didn't go as planned. But I was learning—learning how to adapt, how to solve problems on the fly, and how to turn challenges into more momentum.

Each new event was another chance to refine my approach, to understand what worked and what didn't.

Home of Wolfpack

By the time I transitioned to NC State, my events business was thriving. It wasn't just about the money anymore—it was about the connections I was building and the lessons I was learning along the way. The business forced me to step outside my comfort zone, to put myself out there in ways I never had before.

College became more than just an academic experience—it was a crash course in entrepreneurship, leadership, and resilience. While I didn't have a traditional support system or a safety net, I had something just as powerful: the drive to succeed. My events became a platform for growth—not just for me, but for the people who attended, the DJs who played, and the venues that hosted.

The Takeaway: Hustling With Purpose

Those early days of throwing events taught me lessons I carry with me to this day. Here's what they taught me:

- **Bet on Yourself**
  Taking risks is scary, but the rewards can be life-changing. Trust yourself enough to take the leap.
- **Hustle Is About Consistency**
  Success isn't about one big move—it's about showing up every day, putting in the work, and staying consistent.
- **Relationships Are Everything**
  The connections I made through my events weren't just transactional—they were transformational. Always invest in people.
- **Adapt and Evolve**
  Nothing ever goes perfectly, but every challenge is an opportunity to learn, grow, and adapt.

That first event was more than a party—it was a turning point. It showed me that I didn't have to settle for the hand I'd been dealt. I could build something of my own, one flyer, one handshake, and one event at a time.

CHAPTER 6: HIGH STAKES

The events business was thriving. Word of mouth spread quickly, and every weekend felt like an opportunity to build on the success of the last. My reputation grew not just at NC State but across Raleigh, Chapel Hill, and Duke. People were talking about my events—not just for the music or the crowds but for the energy that came with them. Every flyer I put up, every handshake I made on campus, and every late night spent negotiating with DJs felt worth it. I was making money. I was building something real. But ambition can sometimes outpace judgment.

A Dream Too Big

At the height of this success, an opportunity came my way that seemed too good to be true. A booking agent reached out, claiming to represent none other than Usher—a name that carried weight as one of the biggest R&B stars of the time, known for chart-topping hits like "Yeah!" and "U Got It Bad." Bringing Usher to Raleigh wouldn't just be another notch on my belt; it would catapult my events business into a league of its own.

I had done celebrity events before—booking Ludacris was one of my earlier wins—but this felt different. This was the kind of opportunity that could define a career. Looking back now, I see the red flags: the vague details, the rushed timelines, the high-pressure negotiation tactics. But back then, I was young, hungry, and eager to prove myself. I didn't see a scam—I saw a chance to make history.

The cost? $30,000. A gut-punching figure for a college kid. But I believed in the vision. My dad and my best friend, Sachin, believed in me too. They didn't just cheer from the sidelines—they stepped into the arena with me. My dad offered a significant chunk of the money. Sachin, my ride-or-die, chipped in without hesitation. And I added everything I had.

I wired the money. All of it. And then I waited.

The Crash

The first sign that something was wrong came in the form of silence. Days passed without any confirmation from the "agent." Then weeks. My calls went unanswered. My emails bounced back. Slowly, the crushing realization sank in: I had been scammed.

$30,000. Gone. My father's hard-earned money. Sachin's savings. Every penny I had scraped together.

The weight of it hit me like a freight train. The optimism that had driven me so far now felt like a cruel joke. I felt gutted, like I had let everyone down. My father, who had always believed in my potential. My best friend, who had stood by me without hesitation. Myself, for being so naïve.

I remember sitting in my room, staring at my phone, replaying the events in my head. What had I missed? How could I have been so blind? The shame was suffocating. Each moment of silence from the agent felt like another blow, confirming that I had been duped. My mind raced with what-ifs and self-recriminations. What if I had asked more questions? What if I had been more cautious?

Telling my dad was one of the hardest conversations of my life. He didn't yell or lecture me. He just looked at me with quiet disappointment—a look that cut deeper than words ever could. Sachin, ever the optimist, brushed it off. "It's just money," he said. "We'll make it back."

But for me, it wasn't just money. It was trust. It was the belief people had placed in me. And I felt like I had squandered it. The emotional toll was heavier than the financial loss. The crushing guilt of having involved my father and Sachin in something that ended so poorly weighed on me day and night.

Setback into Strength

That experience taught me something invaluable: *due diligence*. It wasn't enough to be ambitious or hardworking—I needed to be smart. I needed to question, to verify, to ensure that every opportunity was as solid as it seemed. I had to balance vision with vigilance. Dreams, no matter how big, had to be rooted in reality.

But it also taught me about resilience. The world doesn't stop turning because you made a mistake. The bills still come. The sun still rises. And if you want to survive, you have to keep moving.

The first step in rebuilding was the hardest. Every event I organized after that was haunted by the memory of the loss. But I refused to let it define me. I doubled down on my work, determined to make back what I had lost. Slowly but surely, I began to rebuild—not just my finances but my confidence. Each event became another brick in the foundation of the person I was becoming: tougher, smarter, more discerning.

My father, in his quiet way, continued to support me. Sachin, true to form, stayed by my side. Their faith in me didn't waver, even when mine did. And as painful as that chapter was, it became a turning point. It was the first time I truly understood the stakes of entrepreneurship. The highs were exhilarating, but the lows could be devastating. And if I was going to survive in this world, I had to learn to weather both.

The Takeaway: High Stakes, High Lessons

- **Mistakes Are Catalysts, Not Endings**
  What feels like failure in the moment is often just a lesson in disguise. Every fall is an opportunity to rise stronger.
- **Trust but Verify**
  Ambition is important, but so is caution. Always do your homework, ask the hard questions, and trust your instincts.
- **The Importance of a Support System**
  My father and Sachin didn't abandon me when I stumbled. They reminded me that resilience isn't a solo act—it's built on the shoulders of those who believe in you.
- **Keep Moving**
  The only way out of a setback is through it. Learn, adapt, and keep moving forward.

This wasn't just a fall—it was my first mountain peak and my first devastating valley. Looking back, it was the beginning of understanding the philosophy of the second mountain: that true growth often follows the fall. Peaks teach you how high you can go, but valleys are where the real lessons are learned, where character is built, and where resilience takes root.

This wasn't the end of the story; it was the start of understanding that hustling isn't just about climbing—it's about learning to rise again, each time stronger and more prepared for the challenges ahead.

CHAPTER 7: THE GIG

After the Usher debacle, I was left with nothing but lessons and a lingering sting in my gut. That $30,000 mistake wasn't just a financial hit—it was a blow to my confidence. My father and Sachin had been there for me, their belief unwavering, even as I questioned everything I'd worked for. They didn't lecture me or make me feel small; instead, they reminded me of one thing: this was just the beginning.

Those words stuck with me as I returned to the grind. My focus shifted to smaller gigs—college events, parties, and collaborations with local DJs. It wasn't glamorous, but it was steady. Brick by brick, dollar by dollar, I began rebuilding. What I lacked in resources, I made up for in grit and relationships. Every flyer I hung, every handshake I made, felt like a step toward redemption.

Plastering campuses with flyers became my ritual, often done late at night with my partner in cime, Sachin. I hustled the old-school way— shaking hands, building connections, and leveraging every conversation to keep momentum alive. Social media wasn't an option yet; success required literal legwork. It wasn't easy, but each small victory felt like a lifeline.

The Call That Changed Everything

It was during one of these rebuilding phases that the call came. I had stayed in touch with artist management groups—always making sure to leave the door open, even after the Usher debacle. That persistence paid off when one of these managers reached out with a unique opportunity.

Prince was performing at the PNC Arena and was looking to host an intimate after-party. This wasn't a regular gig—it was *the* gig. Prince wasn't just an artist; he was a global icon. The opportunity to partner on something like this felt like validation for all the groundwork I'd been laying.

They were looking for someone who could deliver an upscale, exclusive event to match Prince's legendary status. And they thought of me.

I still remember sitting in my car after that call, overwhelmed by equal parts excitement and fear. This was my shot—not just to rebuild my reputation but to prove that my setbacks didn't define me. I had to make this happen.

Making It Happen

The Prince event wasn't just another job; it was my moment to prove I could deliver on a grander scale. I approached everything with precision, determined to avoid past mistakes. This time, I did my homework. Every contract, every agreement, and every vendor was vetted meticulously.

Finding the right venue was the first hurdle. I needed a boutique space that could balance intimacy with the electric energy of a Prince after-party. After countless visits and negotiations, I secured the perfect spot. Collaborating with top-tier vendors, I ensured every detail—from lighting to sound to branding—was impeccable. This wasn't just an event; it was an experience.

The marketing was just as relentless. I hit the streets, campuses, and clubs, spreading word-of-mouth buzz. Prince's name carried weight, but I knew it was my reputation that would bring everything together. Late nights and early mornings blurred as I worked tirelessly to ensure nothing was left to chance.

The Night That Changed Everything

The night of the event was electric. The upscale nightclub, The Office, buzzed with anticipation as people streamed in, dressed to impress, ready for what they knew would be an unforgettable night. Excitement hung in the air like static electricity, and every detail had come together perfectly—from the lighting that cast a golden glow over the crowd to the sound system that pulsed with life. This wasn't just another event—it was a statement.

Prince arrived in true superstar fashion, stepping out of his limo with the effortless cool that defined him. I escorted him to a private elevated area behind a curtain, where he could observe the entire crowd without being in full view. The room erupted with whispers and speculation. The crowd knew he was there, but the mystique of his presence made the atmosphere even more electric.

What made the night even more surreal was the hilarious moment with Sachin. As we moved through the crowd, people mistook him for Prince. Sachin, always a good sport, played along briefly, basking in the attention as girls flocked to him. Meanwhile, the real Prince remained behind the curtain, exuding an air of mystery and power.

The event was a roaring success. By the end of the night, I handed Sachin a backpack stuffed with tens of thousands of dollars. He quietly made his way to the car, and I stood there, marveling at what we had achieved. It wasn't just the money—though that was staggering for someone my age, only 19—it was the culmination of grit, resilience, and lessons learned from my past mistakes. It was the night I proved to myself that I could rise above failure and create something extraordinary.

Being Resilient

This event marked a turning point. It wasn't just about the money—though the profit gave me breathing room to consider my next steps.

It was about proving to myself that failure didn't define me. It was about learning to pivot, to adapt, and to grow.

Looking back, the Prince event wasn't just a win; it was a catalyst. It taught me that resilience isn't about avoiding failure—it's about using it. Every mistake, every misstep, becomes a stepping stone if you let it.

The Takeaway: Resilience and Redemption

- **Keep the Door Open**
  Relationships are currency. Stay connected, even when things go wrong. You never know which bridge will lead to your next opportunity.
- **Plan With Precision**
  Big dreams require sharp execution. Do your homework, double-check everything, and leave nothing to chance.
- **Celebrate the Comeback**
  Success isn't just about the peaks—it's about how you climb out of the valleys. Celebrate the journey as much as the destination.
- **Resilience Is a Muscle**
  The more you use it, the stronger it gets. Every setback is an opportunity to grow.

This chapter wasn't just about hosting a successful event—it was about redemption. It was about proving to myself and everyone around me that setbacks aren't endings; they're beginnings. The Prince event wasn't just a comeback; it was *the foundation for something much greater*.

CHAPTER 8: BUILDING MY EMPIRE

When I opened Maanjri Lounge in my early twenties, I had no idea how transformative that leap of faith would be. As a senior at NC State University, I was finishing up my degree and dreaming of building my first brick-and-mortar business. I decided I was going to open a lounge—a space that blended relaxation, vibrancy, and community. At just 20 years old, I had to wait to apply for the ABC permit, but that didn't stop me from diving in headfirst.

The name "Maanjri" held a deeply personal significance. In my native tongue, it means a fair-skinned, pretty-eyed girl with cat-like features—a term of endearment and admiration. At the time, I had just started dating Julie, who would later become my wife. Naming my first business after her felt like the perfect grand gesture, a testament to the love and excitement we shared.

I poured my heart into building the concept. Late nights were spent drafting the business plan, sketching ideas, and imagining what the space could be. With the help of my parents, I built the entire lounge with my own two hands—every detail a reflection of the vision I had for something North Carolina had never seen before. Maanjri Lounge wasn't just a hookah bar; it was a manifestation of ambition, innovation, and a willingness to test the unknown.

The idea struck one evening while I was out in Raleigh, observing how people craved unique experiences but often found themselves stuck in repetitive, uninspired spaces. I wanted to create a place where relaxation met vibrancy, where the community could come together in an atmosphere that felt both fresh and familiar. I envisioned the hum of conversation blending with upbeat music, the aroma of hookah weaving through the air, and a vibe that made people linger just a little longer. That vision became the blueprint for Maanjri Lounge, and I was determined to make it work.

But determination alone wasn't enough.

Birth of an Idea

The first six months were grueling. Hookah had an allure that brought in curious customers, but the nature of the experience meant tables weren't turning fast enough to generate sustainable profits. A single hookah could last hours, and with limited seating, it was a constant struggle to make the numbers work. I remember nights when the lounge would open to just a handful of patrons, their interest fading as the novelty wore off. One particularly frustrating evening, after hours of preparation, only two tables were occupied the entire night. I found myself sitting alone after closing, staring at the empty lounge and wondering if I had made a colossal mistake.

It was during one of those long, reflective nights that an idea struck me. What was I overlooking? As a math geek and a problem solver, I started analyzing the demographics around me. That's when it hit me—I was surrounded by universities. NC State, Duke, and Chapel Hill formed a vibrant student ecosystem. Why wasn't I catering directly to them?

The lounge's original name, "Maanjri," while personally meaningful, was difficult for people to pronounce and didn't resonate with the student crowd. I realized I needed something that clicked. That's when the concept of "Pi Bar" emerged. Simple, catchy, and evocative of both college culture and community, the name was inspired by the mathematical symbol and my love for numbers. It felt like the perfect rebranding strategy to attract sororities, fraternities, and students looking for a place to unwind.

With the rebrand, I leaned fully into the student scene. I launched themed nights, added a DJ, and created promotions tailored specifically for college-goers. Flyers went up across campuses, and word of mouth spread quickly. Before long, lines stretched around the block, and the energy inside was electric. What started as a slow grind transformed into a thriving nightlife destination. Pi Bar became the turning point for my hospitality career, showing me the power of adaptation, understanding your audience, and meeting them where they are.

Life in Upper Eschelon

With the success of Pi Bar, my sights grew bigger. The shift from Pi Bar to Mura Sushi wasn't just a business move—it was a leap of faith driven by my growing confidence in hospitality. But let me tell you, it wasn't without its blunders.

At the time, I thought I was a hotshot, ready to conquer the next frontier. I purchased Miro's Sushi, an existing restaurant in North Hills. In hindsight, I probably made the highest offer ever seen for a restaurant of its size. No attorney, no accountant, just me with my unchecked optimism and the conviction that I knew what I was doing. Looking back, it was a textbook "what not to do" moment, and honestly, I cringe every time I think about it.

But here's the thing about being young and clueless—you don't know what you don't know, and sometimes, that ignorance drives you to take risks others might shy away from. Despite the overpayment, I was determined to make it work. I quickly rolled up my sleeves and got to work applying the principles I'd honed at Pi Bar: know your audience, adapt to meet their needs, and create an experience people can't stop talking about.

In just over a year, I transformed the restaurant from doing $1.5 million in annual revenue to over $3 million. The formula wasn't revolutionary, but it worked: focus on the customer experience, create a sleek and modern ambiance, and empower the staff to deliver exceptional service. Mura wasn't just about sushi—it was about creating moments people would remember.

One particularly chaotic night stands out. The kitchen was running behind, tempers flared, and customers were growing impatient. I stepped in, calming the team and addressing the guests personally. By the end of the night, we'd turned it around. That experience taught me the importance of leadership under pressure and the value of owning every part of the customer experience.

Mura wasn't just a restaurant; it became a brand. Its modern, sleek atmosphere, carefully curated menu, and exceptional customer service set it apart. Every detail, from the elegant presentation of the sushi to the attentive staff, was designed to create a memorable dining experience. The ambiance was both upscale and inviting, with dim lighting and contemporary decor that made guests feel they were part of something special. These elements together made Mura a staple in Raleigh, redefining what a sushi restaurant could be. It wasn't just about serving food—it was about creating an experience.

The journey to Mura was a humbling reminder of what ambition without preparation can lead to. But it also showed me the power of adaptability. Despite the missteps, I learned how to rinse and repeat the principles that worked: understanding your audience, delivering value, and leveraging your team's strengths. Those lessons didn't just fuel Mura's success—they set the foundation for what would come next.

In 2008, I formalized my ventures under Eschelon Experience. Eschelon wasn't just a collection of venues—it was an ethos, a blueprint for delivering excellence across every aspect of hospitality.

Over the next decade, Eschelon Experiences grew into a hospitality powerhouse in the Triangle. By its peak, we had more than 1,000 employees and were generating millions in annual revenue. But scaling wasn't just about opening more doors—it was about creating a culture.

Each concept we launched had its own identity. From Mura's contemporary dining experience to more niche concepts that appealed to targeted demographics, Eschelon became synonymous with innovation and excellence. We didn't just open venues; we crafted destinations.

The numbers told part of the story, but the bigger success lay in the emotional connections we built. Eschelon wasn't just about the business; it was about people. The team members who believed in the vision, the guest who trusted us to create memorable experiences, and the community that supported us.

Leadership Under Fire

Running a hospitality empire came with its share of hard lessons. One moment stands out vividly in my memory. During a particularly challenging week, a key manager at one of our busiest venues handed in their resignation, citing burnout and feeling undervalued. It was a wake-up call for me. I realized that while I was focused on scaling the business and hitting revenue targets, I had overlooked the well-being of the very people who made those successes possible.

Rather than rushing to fill the position, I sat down with the manager and asked what had gone wrong. Their honesty was humbling. They talked about the pressure, the lack of acknowledgment, and how their hard work often felt invisible. That conversation sparked a shift in my approach to leadership. I began prioritizing regular check-ins with my team, implementing systems to celebrate wins—big and small—and creating a culture where employees felt seen and supported.

Scaling a hospitality empire also demanded replicable systems. From kitchen operations to HR practices, it quickly became clear that consistency and structure were essential to maintain quality across multiple venues. Leadership wasn't optional either; managing a team of 1,000 employees required inspiring, delegating, and fostering accountability. One defining moment was coaching a struggling manager, helping them regain their confidence and, in turn, elevate the entire team.

The hospitality industry's volatility made staying ahead of trends a constant challenge. What's trendy today can be outdated tomorrow. Adapting to these shifts required relentless curiosity and innovation. One of the most pivotal moments in Eschelon's journey came during the early 2010s when competition in Raleigh's hospitality scene surged. New venues were opening left and right, and customer expectations were higher than ever. Instead of retreating, I doubled down, using data to understand our customers better, revamping menus, and elevating overall experiences. It wasn't just about staying relevant—it was about staying indispensable.

Community Impact

Beyond profits, Eschelon's true legacy was its impact on the community. I have always believed that building a company is never a solo act—it takes a village. The unwavering support of the community made Eschelon possible, and giving back has always been vital to our mission. One of my core philosophies is simple: if you have, then give, and when you feel like you can't give anymore, give just a little bit more.

Eschelon provided thousands of jobs, supported local vendors, and became a key player in Raleigh's economic growth. But our work went far beyond numbers. Hosting fundraisers, supporting local causes, and using our platform to uplift others became the heart of our mission.

One moment stands out: organizing a community dinner during the holiday season. The energy that night was electric. Families arrived in waves, each greeted with warm smiles and the aroma of freshly prepared meals. We partnered with local charities to make it happen, transforming one of our venues into a vibrant, welcoming space filled with laughter and connection. I remember walking through the room, seeing kids sharing stories, parents relaxing over plates of food, and volunteers working tirelessly to ensure every guest felt at home.

That night wasn't just a dinner—it was a reflection of everything Eschelon stood for: creating spaces where people feel seen, valued, and connected. It was a reminder of why I started in hospitality. This industry isn't just about running successful venues; it's about building a community, one meal and one memory at a time. The impact of that evening lingered long after the plates were cleared, solidifying our commitment to give back. For me, hospitality will always be about the people—bringing them together, fostering connection, and creating a legacy of care and gratitude. That night reminded me why I started in hospitality. It wasn't just about running successful venues; it was about building a community, one meal and one memory at a time. Watching people come together, sharing food and stories, reinforced the purpose that fueled every concept we built—to bring people together in meaningful ways.

Takeaways: Lessons from Building an Empire

- **Build with Purpose:** Every concept needs a clear vision. Customers don't just want products; they want experiences.
- **Invest in People:** Your employees are your greatest asset. Empower them, support them, and they'll drive your vision forward.
- **Pivot, Always:** Hospitality requires adaptability. Whether it's shifting a concept or revamping operations, staying rigid is a recipe for failure.
- **Know Your Market:** Data is a powerful tool. Understanding customer behavior and market trends allowed us to stay ahead.
- **Create Community:** Success isn't just about profits—it's about impact. Building relationships with customers, employees, and the community creates a foundation that lasts.

Here is the simple truth: success is built on the lessons learned from both wins and failures. Each venture carried its own challenges, but the common thread was *adaptability and resilience*. From rebranding to connect with a new audience to doubling down on leadership during tough times, these experiences shaped a deeper understanding of what it takes to build not just a business, but a legacy. At its core, hospitality is about people—bringing them together, creating memories, and making an impact that goes beyond the bottom line.

What these experiences taught me is that entrepreneurship is never linear. It's messy, unpredictable, and often humbling. But within that chaos lies the opportunity for greatness. Every setback carries the seed of reinvention, and every success offers a chance to elevate others along the way.

Building an empire isn't about the numbers; it's about the legacy you leave—the lives you touch, the communities you strengthen, and the memories you help create. And for me, that will always be the true measure of success.

CHAPTER 9: THE PINNACLE BEFORE THE PLUNGE

The music was deafening, reverberating through the floors and pounding in my chest like a second heartbeat. A DJ spun tracks from a neon-lit booth, their movements synchronized with the crowd's energy as each bass drop sent a ripple of euphoria through the packed room. The crowd roared, hands raised high, faces illuminated by flashing strobe lights, and the sheer intensity of the moment was almost tangible—an intoxicating blend of chaos and unity. The line outside the club snaked around the block, a spectacle of high heels, sharp suits, and gleaming luxury cars parked haphazardly in front. Inside, my staff moved like a well-oiled machine—bartenders flipping bottles in choreographed precision, servers weaving effortlessly through the throng of patrons, and the hum of cash registers barely audible over the roar of the crowd.

This wasn't just a good night; this was the culmination of everything I'd built. The dream realized. Standing there amidst the vibrant chaos, I felt a wave of pride and disbelief. This was the vision I had nurtured through countless sleepless nights, the risks I had taken when the odds seemed insurmountable. Yet, as I soaked in the applause of a bustling crowd and the precision of a team operating at its peak, a quiet voice in the back of my mind whispered:

"What's next?"

The satisfaction was fleeting, tinged with the weight of expectation and the haunting realization that reaching the pinnacle often meant the climb had only begun. Echelon Experiences had become the pinnacle of hospitality in Raleigh and beyond, synonymous with innovation, elegance, and the kind of nightlife that attracted celebrities and locals alike. My venues were at full capacity nightly, accolades flowed in, and revenue streams were growing month over month. On the surface, everything looked flawless.

But deep down, I knew the truth: this level of success was a double-edged sword. It wasn't just the empire I'd built; it was the weight of carrying it on my shoulders.

The Cost of the Dream

Success wasn't without its toll. There were nights I barely slept, lying awake with a phone in one hand and a spreadsheet in the other, troubleshooting operational hiccups and financial projections. The industry thrived on relentless energy and constant reinvention, and while my competitors scrambled to catch up, I knew I couldn't afford to stand still.

To keep Eschelon on top, I was constantly pitching new concepts, brokering partnerships, and securing funding. Each new project seemed like a logical step forward: more venues, bigger investments, bolder visions. But there were limits, and I was starting to feel them.

The cracks began subtly—projects that stretched thin on resources, strained relationships with staff, or budgets that needed creative maneuvering to stay on track. Then there was the mounting pressure to maintain a public persona of infallibility, a smiling face in interviews and public appearances, even as the cracks behind the scenes began to grow wider.

A Friday Night Reality Check

One Friday night, as I stood in the VIP section of one of my venues, surrounded by investors and local celebrities, I felt a momentary pang of disconnection. The laughter and animated conversations around me felt distant, muffled by the weight in my chest. I sipped a drink and stared at the vibrant energy below—the packed dance floor, the pulsing lights, the sheer spectacle of it all—and yet, I couldn't shake the hollow ache creeping in. It was as if I were an outsider in the very world I had created, questioning if this was what fulfillment was supposed to feel like.

"This is what you wanted," I reminded myself. But the question that lingered was: "At what cost?"

It wasn't just the sleepless nights or the endless hustle. It was missing family dinners, friends growing distant, and relationships that felt increasingly transactional. For every deal closed and milestone achieved, there was something intangible slipping further from my grasp.

The First Signs of Overextension

The first real red flag came with a location that seemed destined for success—Oberlin Road and Clark Avenue, an intersection many considered the heartbeat of Raleigh's growth. The area was undergoing a massive redevelopment, and I saw it as the perfect opportunity to anchor Eschelon at the epicenter of the city's evolution. Riding high on the momentum of a dozen successful ventures, I approached this project with unshaken confidence, convinced it couldn't fail.

The concept was ambitious: a hybrid venue that combined high-end dining with an upscale nightlife experience, something Raleigh hadn't seen before. On paper, it looked flawless. The numbers projected high returns and immediate buzz, promising to elevate Eschelon into uncharted territory. But looking back, it was a classic case of ambition outpacing preparation.

Without proper due diligence, I moved forward, putting all my eggs in one basket. What I didn't account for was the complexity of the market and the reality of consumer behavior. The project began to stretch—over time, over budget, and beyond its original scope. Securing the location turned out to be more costly than anticipated, and the design phase became a quagmire of revisions and delays. Staffing shortages hit hard, compounding the already mounting challenges. What should have been a golden opportunity quickly turned into a logistical nightmare.

At that point, I had yet to experience a true failure in my entrepreneurial journey. Each prior success had bolstered my confidence, reinforcing the belief that hard work alone could overcome any obstacle. But this project became a cautionary tale— forcing me to confront the risks of overextension, the dangers of unchecked ambition, and the fragility of leadership stretched too thin. It wasn't just a missed opportunity; it was the first time I saw the weight of my choices threatening to topple everything I had built.

A Personal Toll

On the surface, I maintained the façade of someone in control. My public persona was polished, confident, and charismatic. But in private, I was beginning to fray. The stress manifested physically— headaches, fatigue, and a constant knot in my stomach. Mentally, the doubts began to creep in: Was I pushing too hard? Was I losing sight of why I'd started this journey in the first place?

One night, after closing out the books for the month, I sat in my office long after the last staff member had left. The silence was deafening. I stared at the glowing numbers on the screen—profits, expenses, projections—and felt a wave of exhaustion wash over me.

"Is this it?" I thought. "Is this what success is supposed to feel like?" The question lingered like a heavy fog, forcing me to confront the disconnect between my achievements and my sense of purpose. In that moment, I realized I had been so focused on climbing that I hadn't prepared for the weight of standing at the summit. Success had become a moving target, and I needed to re-evaluate—not just my professional goals, but what truly mattered in my life.

-

Takeaway: The Hidden Weight of Success

- **The Illusion of the Summit**: Success often appears as the ultimate goal, but reaching the top can reveal new challenges and pressures. It's essential to prepare not just for the climb but for sustaining yourself once you arrive.
- **Burnout is Real**: Ambition and hard work are necessary, but unchecked, they can lead to burnout. Entrepreneurs must learn to balance their drive with self-care and boundaries.
- **Recalibrate Your Focus**: As businesses grow, it's easy to lose sight of the original mission. Periodically revisit your "why" to ensure you're aligned with your values and vision.
- **The Power of Saying No**: Not every opportunity is the right opportunity. Success often comes from making strategic choices about where to direct your energy and resources.
- **Invest in Relationships**: The journey to the top can strain personal and professional relationships. Prioritize those connections and ensure the people in your life feel valued, not overlooked.

Success isn't just about reaching the pinnacle; it's about understanding how to carry the weight once you're there. The climb may be exhilarating, but the true test lies in finding balance, staying true to your purpose, and remembering that the summit is only part of the journey.

CHAPTER 10: THE CRACKS WIDEN

The first sign of collapse came with a call from my CFO. I was in my office, reviewing plans for yet another expansion, when my phone buzzed. The tone of their voice immediately made my stomach drop.

"We can't make payroll," they said, and those words hit like a sledgehammer.

My mind raced, trying to process the gravity of what this meant. Without the funds to pay my employees, everything else—operations, buying food, running the venues—felt like it would unravel.

For months, we'd been siphoning cash and profits from successful ventures to keep struggling ones afloat. It was a balancing act I thought I could manage, but this moment shattered that illusion. The news rippled through the organization, and the effects were immediate. Vendors began calling about late payments, deliveries were delayed, and morale plummeted. At one location, the head chef walked out mid-shift, leaving the kitchen scrambling to cover orders. Servers whispered anxiously in break rooms, and managers faced angry questions they couldn't answer.

The cracks weren't just in the spreadsheets; they were in the spirit of the team. This wasn't just a financial setback—it was a cultural one. When you can't pay your people, trust erodes, faith dwindles, and the very foundation of what you've built begins to shake. It was the first domino in a series of events that would threaten to bring everything crashing down.

Ambition Meets Reality

The hospitality industry is notoriously volatile, and my business was no exception. Seasonal fluctuations and rising labor costs had already made growth more challenging. But now, a looming economic downturn began to affect consumer spending habits. Diners were less inclined to splurge on luxury experiences, and nightlife attendance waned.

Managing multiple venues became increasingly demanding, with each location requiring unique attention—from staffing to marketing. What had once symbolized ambition now felt like a precarious balancing act. High turnover and burnout among staff exacerbated the challenges, while replacing key team members drained already limited resources. These operational strains exposed vulnerabilities I had previously overlooked, leaving little margin for error in an industry already prone to volatility.

These pressures coalesced into a perfect storm, testing the limits of both my business and my leadership.

Doubts in the Silence

One particularly rough night, I walked into one of my venues and immediately sensed something was off. The usual buzz of lively conversation and clinking glasses was replaced with muted chatter and an eerie quiet. The music felt flat, as if it was struggling to fill the space, and fewer patrons lingered at the bar or on the dance floor. I stood at the bar, sipping a drink, and watched as my staff moved with a noticeable tension—smiles forced, movements hurried but without their usual rhythm. Their body language told the story: they were tired, overworked, and fighting to keep the night running smoothly. It was clear that the strain wasn't just operational—it reflected a deeper crack in the leadership that once energized them.

That night, I stayed long after the doors closed. Sitting alone in the dimly lit venue, I could hear the faint hum of the refrigerators and the occasional clatter of glassware being cleaned in the back. The silence felt deafening, amplifying the doubts that had been creeping in. This wasn't just about the business; it was about the people who relied on me. Employees, vendors, partners—all part of a larger ecosystem I had created, now on the verge of collapse. The visible exhaustion of my staff weighed heavily on me. I had built an empire, but for the first time, I questioned if I had the strength—or the insight—to keep it from falling apart.

Hard Choices, Lasting Lessons

Scaling back meant making some of the hardest decisions of my career. Closing a venue was like losing a part of myself. Each concept was born from a vision, nurtured with creativity and sweat equity. But business isn't about sentimentality—it's about survival.

We made the call to shutter two locations. Breaking the news to the team was gut-wrenching. I called a meeting and stood before a room of confused and fearful faces. My voice trembled as I explained the situation. The hardest part was knowing that my words couldn't erase their pain.

By consolidating resources, we aimed to stabilize the remaining venues. It was a painful but necessary step. The closures reshaped my decision-making moving forward, teaching me that survival often requires sacrifice and that every ending carries the seed of a new beginning.

The Personal Toll

As the business struggled, so did my personal life. Long hours and constant stress strained my relationships. One evening, my youngest daughter walked into my office, clutching a drawing.

"When will you come play with us again?" she asked. Her words cut through me, and I realized how much I stood to lose.

Moments later, my wife entered, placing a hand on my shoulder. "We'll get through this," she said softly. Her words were a lifeline, but the drawing underscored the stakes. I realized I needed to rebuild—not just the business but also myself and my relationships.

Takeaway: Lessons from the Edge

- **Embrace Humility:** Growth is exciting, but unchecked ambition can lead to overextension. Learn to recognize your limits and adjust before the cracks widen.
- **Focus on Sustainability:** It's not just about scaling up; it's about ensuring that growth is manageable and sustainable. Sometimes, less is more.
- **Listen to Your Team:** As a leader, it's easy to get caught up in your vision. But your team's feedback is invaluable. They're in the trenches and often see problems before you do.
- **Prioritize Relationships:** Success is meaningless if it comes at the cost of your relationships. Make time for the people who matter, even in the midst of chaos.
- **Adapt and Rebuild:** Challenges are inevitable, but how you respond defines your path forward. Don't be afraid to pivot, let go of failing ventures, and focus on what's truly important.

Success isn't just about how high you climb; it's about how well you can weather the fall. This chapter wasn't just about survival—it was about recalibration, learning to embrace change, and rediscovering what truly matters.

CHAPTER 11: THE UNRAVELING

A Ship Taking on Water

The unraveling of my hospitality empire wasn't a singular moment; it was the inevitable fallout of decisions and challenges that had been brewing for years. Tied directly to the struggles outlined in the previous chapters—missed payrolls, declining morale, and overextension—it marked the slow and excruciating dismantling of everything I had built. What began as a dream had become a relentless nightmare. It was as if I was a passenger on a ship taking on water, desperately trying to bail it out while the cracks multiplied beneath me. Each day felt like another wave crashing over me, pushing me closer to the abyss.

The first warning signs had been subtle—a slow decline in foot traffic, an uptick in vendor calls about late payments—but I ignored them, chalking it up to the usual ebbs and flows of the industry. I was too proud, too focused on growth, to realize the foundation was starting to crack. What kept me pushing forward, even as the cracks widened, was the belief that hard work and persistence could fix anything. That belief, while well-intentioned, blinded me to the fact that sometimes stepping back is the only way forward.

The Initial Cracks

The reality hit me during a routine meeting with my CFO, where the stark truth was laid bare.

"Gaurav, we're running dangerously close to zero in reserves," he said, sliding the cash flow statement across the table. The numbers were sobering—a clear indicator that the business was on the brink.

I forced myself to maintain composure, but inside, panic was clawing at me. "What's the next step?" I finally asked, trying to keep the tremor out of my voice.

"We need to act now," he replied firmly. "Cut back operations, close underperforming venues, renegotiate leases—or we won't make it to the end of the quarter."

His words hung heavy in the room, each suggestion a painful reminder of how far things had spiraled. I nodded slowly, pretending to process the recommendations, but my mind was elsewhere. I couldn't stop thinking about what all this would mean for my team, my family, and the dream I had poured everything into. It was a moment of clarity, but also one of deep personal reckoning.

The Domino Effect

The first major blow came from one of our anchor venues—a location that had been a cornerstone of our brand but was now struggling to break even. The eviction notice hit the team hard, sparking a wave of uncertainty among staff. Conversations once filled with camaraderie turned into whispers of doubt. Long-time employees, who had helped build the venue's success, expressed feelings of betrayal and fear for their future. For our loyal customers, the closure felt personal. Some wrote emails sharing their heartbreak over losing a space where they had celebrated milestones, while others vented frustration at the sudden end. The human cost of this loss reverberated far beyond the financials, shaking the trust and community we had worked so hard to cultivate.

The letter arrived on a rainy Tuesday afternoon. It was short and to the point: eviction proceedings would begin unless we paid the overdue rent in full within 30 days. I remember holding the letter, my hands trembling, as the rain tapped against the office window. This wasn't just a venue—it was my reputation, my legacy. Losing it felt unthinkable.

But the hits kept coming. Vendors began cutting us off, unwilling to extend further credit. The seafood supplier was the first, followed by the liquor distributor. Suddenly, the menus we prided ourselves on became liabilities. Without key ingredients, we had to make substitutions, cutting corners in ways that betrayed everything I had built.

The Personal Costs

Julie had always been my greatest supporter, but even she struggled to understand the depths of what I was going through. Her unwavering presence, however, became a quiet but powerful force during this period. While she voiced her frustrations about the toll my work was taking on our family, her steadfast belief in my ability to overcome became a grounding anchor. Her honesty pushed me to reflect on the choices I was making, not just for the business but for the people I loved most. Through her balance of support and accountability, Julie influenced my decisions to start prioritizing health, relationships, and eventually, a new vision for what success could look like. Our late-night talks became arguments, her patience wearing thin as I withdrew further into myself.

"You can't keep doing this, Gaurav," she said one night, her voice breaking. "You're not just losing the business—you're losing us."

I wanted to reassure her, to promise that things would get better, but the words wouldn't come. How could I promise what I no longer believed?

The stress began to manifest physically. Sleep became a luxury I couldn't afford, and when I did manage to rest, I woke up drenched in sweat, my heart racing. My diet consisted of whatever I could grab between meetings—usually something fried or sugary to keep me going. I started skipping doctor's appointments, ignoring the warning signs my body was sending me.

One night, the chest pains became unbearable. I was sitting in the office, staring at yet another stack of unpaid bills, when the pain hit like a freight train. It radiated down my arm, making it hard to breathe. Julie rushed me to the ER, where the doctor confirmed what I had feared: I was on the verge of a heart attack.

"You need to slow down," he said. "Your body can't sustain this level of stress."

But slowing down felt impossible. The business demanded more of me than ever, and stepping back felt like giving up.

The Breaking Point

The final blow came in the form of a lawsuit from one of my investors. The accusations weren't entirely baseless—I had taken risks that hadn't paid off, and the cracks in the business were undeniable. But the lawsuit went beyond the financial strain; it felt deeply personal, as though my character and intentions were under attack. The local press latched onto the story, painting me as reckless and irresponsible. Headlines like "Hospitality Mogul Faces Lawsuit Amid Financial Turmoil" tarnished the reputation I had worked so hard to build. Sitting in the courtroom, I couldn't help but feel like I was watching the erosion of not just my business, but my identity as a leader. It forced me to confront the painful reality that leadership is not just about vision—it's about accountability, and in this case, I had fallen short.

The lawsuit was a humbling experience, forcing me to reevaluate what leadership truly meant. It wasn't just about inspiring others or creating something grand—it was about owning my mistakes and rebuilding trust, both with myself and those around me. This painful realization planted the first seeds of change, preparing me for the rebuilding phase that lay ahead.

The Seeds of a New Beginning

Amid the wreckage, there were moments of clarity—small glimmers of hope that reminded me of why I had started this journey. One such moment came during a quiet evening when I received a message from a long-time customer. It read: "Your venue was where I met my spouse. I just wanted you to know how much that space meant to us and so many others." That simple note brought tears to my eyes. It reminded me that even as things fell apart, the connections and memories I had helped create still lived on. It was these reminders, however small, that kept me grounded and gave me the resilience to imagine a way forward.

Julie, despite the strain on our relationship, never stopped believing in me. One night, as we sat on the porch in silence, she took my hand and said, "You're more than this, Gaurav. This is just a chapter, not the whole story." Her words reframed my perspective and helped me start envisioning a new path forward.

Industry Insights: The High-Stakes World of Hospitality

The hospitality industry is one of the most volatile sectors in the world, and I've lived that reality firsthand. From navigating razor-thin margins to juggling labor costs and customer expectations, the stakes were always high. I remember one month in particular when a delayed seafood shipment forced us to rewrite our menu overnight, leading to frustrated customers and unexpected revenue losses. It was a stark reminder that resilience and adaptability aren't optional—they're essential for survival. Margins are razor-thin, competition is fierce, and customer expectations are ever-changing. According to industry reports:

- Approximately 60% of new restaurants fail within the first year.
- Labor costs account for an average of 30% of revenue, leaving little room for error.

- Rising real estate costs and supply chain disruptions have become major challenges, particularly in urban markets.

For entrepreneurs, the lesson is clear: the hospitality business is not for the faint of heart. Success requires not just passion but meticulous planning, financial discipline, and the ability to adapt to an ever-changing landscape.

Takeaways: Lessons from the Unraveling

- **Grow Strategically, Not Recklessly:** Expansion is exciting, but it can also be your downfall. Focus on sustainable growth, ensuring you have the infrastructure and cash flow to support it.
- **Build a Financial Safety Net:** In a volatile industry, reserves are your lifeline. Plan for the unexpected because the unexpected will come.
- **Separate Your Identity from Your Business:** It's easy to tie your self-worth to your success, but your value is not determined by P&L statements.
- **Embrace Failure as a Catalyst:** Setbacks are not the end— they're opportunities to learn, pivot, and come back stronger.
- **Prioritize Your Health and Relationships:** No business is worth sacrificing your well-being or the people you love. Make time for self-care and nurture your personal connections.
- **Be Transparent with Your Team:** Your employees are your greatest asset. Keep them informed, involve them in problem-solving, and show them you value their contributions.

Final Thoughts

The unraveling of my hospitality empire was one of the most profound periods of transformation in my life. What began with ambition and boundless energy eventually led me to the crucible of missed payrolls, strained relationships, and public scrutiny. But from that crucible emerged growth, clarity, and purpose. This journey forced me to redefine leadership, not as a position of power, but as a commitment to accountability, humility, and resilience.

Through these chapters, one truth has become clear: moments of collapse are not just endings; they are beginnings. They strip away pretenses, exposing what truly matters. For me, it was relationships—with my team, my family, and myself—that became the foundation for rebuilding. Leadership isn't about perfection; it's about adaptability and the courage to rise after being broken apart.

If there is one overarching reflection from this section, it is this: what the world calls failure, I now call a catalyst. These moments of challenge are invitations to evolve, to rethink, and to rewrite. Standing at rock bottom, I found the strength to recalibrate my life, to let go of what wasn't serving me, and to nurture the seeds of a new vision.

Rock bottom isn't the end—it's your restart. Use it to rebuild with integrity, purpose, and strength. Because every crack, every misstep, is a doorway to something greater. In the next phase, I will share how those seeds took root, and how I redefined success on my terms, not the world's.

CHAPTER 12: THE CATALYST FOR REINVENTION

The fall came like a tidal wave, starting with a devastating phone call during a board meeting. "The Triangle Business Journal just published the article," my partner said. In that instant, years of hard work unraveled. My thriving hospitality empire, once a source of pride, now felt like an anchor pulling me under. The loss was more than financial—it was deeply personal. The connections I had built, the dreams I had turned into reality, and the identity I had crafted were now in ruins. The thriving hospitality empire, once a source of pride and a testament to my entrepreneurial spirit, now felt like a weight dragging me under. The loss was more than financial—it was personal. I had poured my soul into creating a brand that connected people, provided jobs, and turned dreams into reality. And now, it was gone.

I sat alone in the silence, the echo of everything I'd lost ringing in my ears. What stung most wasn't just the financial collapse—it was the faces of the people I felt I had let down. Employees who had depended on me for stability. Friends and family who had believed in my vision. Myself, who once dared to think I could conquer it all.

But rock bottom has a way of forcing clarity. For me, it came during one of those late-night walks, when I finally stopped running from my thoughts and faced them head-on. I realized that I'd been building my life on a foundation that no longer served me, and it was time to start over—with purpose. For the first time in years, I wasn't buried in the daily grind or swept up in the next venture. I was just...still. It was terrifying at first, but in that stillness, I found something I hadn't had in a long time: *perspective*.

Reflecting on the Fall

Failure, as society defines it, is supposed to feel final—an unchangeable verdict that marks the end of the road. But the truth is, failure can be the most powerful teacher. It forces you to confront your deepest fears and reassess the path that led you there. For me, it wasn't the act of failing that carried the heaviest weight; it was the internalized shame and judgment I allowed to define me. This wasn't the end, though—it was a catalyst, an unanticipated opportunity to reassess and rewrite my story.

The loss made me face hard truths about the life I had built. I had been running so fast that I hadn't stopped to ask whether the foundation I was building on aligned with my values or my long-term vision. The collapse gave me no choice but to pause and reevaluate. Accountability became my ally—not a weight to carry but a tool to reclaim control.

Hitting Pause

Hitting pause is not just an act of stopping; it's an intentional choice to recalibrate. When my world crumbled, my instinct was to rebuild as quickly as possible, to mask the pain with distractions and action. But I realized that rushing forward without clarity would only perpetuate the same cycles that led to my downfall. Hitting pause meant stepping into the discomfort of stillness, facing the wreckage of my life, and shedding the layers of identity that no longer fit.

Letting go was the hardest part. I stepped back from the parties, the networking events, and the superficial relationships that had defined my success. It felt like surrender, but it was transformation in disguise. The shedding of old habits and roles wasn't about loss; it was about creating space for something new to emerge. On late-night walks, as the cool air grounded me, I began to untangle my thoughts. Journaling became my lifeline, a way to pour out the chaos and reconnect with the values I had long ignored. In that stillness, I rediscovered the purpose that had been buried under years of ambition and noise.

Reassessing Identity and Purpose

Who are you when the accolades fade and the roles dissolve? This haunting question lay at the heart of my struggle, forcing me to confront the uncomfortable truths I'd avoided for so long. For years, my identity had been wrapped tightly around external markers of success—the titles, the ventures, the perception of being the person who had it all figured out. Without them, I felt unmoored, like a ship without a compass.

In those silent moments of reflection, I began asking myself deeper questions: Who am I when no one is watching? What values truly drive me? What does success mean if it doesn't align with the core of who I am? These weren't fleeting curiosities—they were unrelenting interrogations that demanded honesty and patience. They didn't come with neat answers, only raw truths waiting to be uncovered.

I realized that the fire inside me, once a raging inferno of ambition, had dimmed to a barely flickering ember. But even in its faintest glow, it was still there, whispering to me that it could burn again. Reassessing my identity wasn't about reclaiming the old fire—it was about understanding how to nurture it back to life in a way that aligned with my deeper values and purpose.

Purpose, I discovered, is not an external destination. It's not found in titles, applause, or societal approval. It's something internal—a quiet, steady force that comes from living in alignment with your core values. As Viktor Frankl wrote in Man's Search for Meaning, "When we are no longer able to change a situation, we are challenged to change ourselves." That's what this journey was: a challenge to redefine success and significance on my own terms.

This reassessment didn't provide instant clarity; instead, it refined the questions that guided me forward. Are you living for approval, or are you living for authenticity? Are your pursuits driven by genuine passion, or are they distractions from the truths you're afraid to face? What legacy are you creating, and does it truly reflect the person you aspire to be?

These questions are not meant to be answered in one sitting; they're meant to linger, to provoke thought, and to spark a journey of self-discovery. They are the threads that pull you closer to your authentic self. For me, answering them was about rediscovering the faint ember inside me and learning to protect it from the winds of doubt and distraction.

Reassessing identity and purpose isn't a one-time exercise. It's a lifelong process of peeling back layers, shedding what no longer serves you, and stepping into the next version of yourself. The ember grew into a steady flame, not because I found all the answers, but because I dared to keep asking the questions that mattered. And in that steady flame, I found clarity, resilience, and the courage to move forward.

Starting Small: Rebuilding One Step at a Time

Rebuilding didn't happen overnight. The first and most crucial step was taking inventory of my core values. What truly mattered to me? What principles did I want my life and work to reflect? Identifying these core values became my foundation. Without them, I realized, everything else—success, purpose, clarity—was precarious and unsustainable.

Core values act as an internal compass, guiding decisions and keeping us balanced. When you deviate from them, you're like a ship drifting off course, lost in a sea of distractions. For me, rebuilding meant reestablishing these values as my anchor. It required deep introspection and a willingness to question everything I'd prioritized before.

To uncover your own core values, start small. Reflect on moments in your life that brought you fulfillment—what was present? When have you felt the most disconnected, and what values were missing? Your values are the non-negotiables that align your internal world with your external actions. They're your truth, and while they may evolve over time, they remain the bedrock of your identity.

With my values defined, I began reconnecting with my network, not to pitch ideas but to listen and learn. I reached out to mentors and former colleagues, people who had weathered their own storms and come out stronger. Their advice wasn't just practical—it was inspiring.

I also focused on the basics. What skills could I sharpen? What knowledge gaps could I fill? I invested in myself, attending workshops, reading voraciously, and learning from every source I could find. Each small win—whether it was mastering a new skill or having a productive conversation—felt like a brick in the foundation of my comeback.

The Role of Support Systems

If there's one thing I learned during this period, it's the power of support. In my darkest moments, my instinct was to push everyone away. I convinced myself that nobody truly had my best interests at heart, that I was better off dealing with the fallout alone. But that was far from the truth. What I discovered was that a genuine support system isn't just about being there during the good times—it's about standing beside you when you're at your lowest, refusing to let you fall further.

Over the years, I'd amassed countless connections—thousands of acquaintances and colleagues who called themselves friends. But in those moments of crisis, I realized that the number of people who truly mattered could be counted on one hand. These were the individuals who didn't just stand by me but actively challenged me when I started to stray from my path, even as I was attempting to rebuild myself.

One late night, when I was spiraling in self-doubt, my mother sat beside me and said quietly, "You don't have to figure it all out right now, but you do have to start." Her simple wisdom grounded me, reminding me that progress isn't about leaps—it's about steps. Similarly, my wife's unwavering encouragement became my anchor. She refused to let me define myself by my failures. "You're more than this moment," she said, cutting through the noise of self-criticism. "You've come back from worse, and you'll come back from this."

Support isn't about saying what you want to hear; it's about saying what you need to hear. My closest friends held me accountable, calling out my blind spots and reminding me of the core values I had established. They weren't afraid to be honest, even when it hurt, because they saw the bigger picture—the person I could become.

I also began to see support systems as more than just people who lift you up. They are mirrors reflecting back the parts of yourself that you might overlook or ignore. Their presence brought clarity to my journey, reminding me of my purpose and reinforcing the belief that I wasn't defined by my setbacks but by how I responded to them.

In the end, my support system wasn't vast, but it was mighty. They were my foundation, helping me rediscover who I truly was and guiding me toward the person I was meant to be. This period taught me that true support isn't about quantity—it's about quality. It's about having those few people who stand by you, unwavering, when the world feels like it's falling apart.

Laying the Foundation for the Next Chapter

As I began to rediscover myself, the next chapter of my life took an unexpected turn with the arrival of two people who would become pivotal to my journey: Vincenzo and Nikita. At the time, I was still trying to piece together what my future might look like—poking around, exploring ideas, and searching for clarity. What I found instead was a brotherhood.

Meeting Vincenzo and Nikita wasn't entirely by chance. I had crossed paths with both through my career in hospitality, where I had built connections that spanned industries. Vincenzo and Nikita, however, were deeply rooted in the world of commercial real estate—a path they had been practicing for years. In 2019, their vision aligned, and they decided to launch their own flag, City Plat Commercial Real Estate, alongside their third partner, Pat. Although I hadn't met Pat before this chapter of my life, he had been working closely with Vincenzo and Nikita, bringing his own expertise and dedication to the table. Together, the three of them created a powerful synergy that laid the foundation for what would become a transformative journey for all of us.

What made our connection unique was the honesty. There was no sugarcoating, no pretense. Vincenzo and Nikita called me out when I veered off course, pushing me to stay aligned with the core values I was beginning to redefine. In turn, I learned to listen, to reflect, and to grow through their insights. Together, we began laying the groundwork for something significant—a new chapter built not just on ambition but on purpose, connection, and shared belief.

This wasn't about chasing opportunities for the sake of it. It was about building with intention, about creating something that resonated deeply with who I was becoming. Vincenzo, Nikita, and Pat helped me see that the next chapter wasn't just about rebuilding what I had lost; it was about reimagining what I could create, with clarity and conviction guiding every step forward.

What I came to understand during this time was the importance of leaning into discomfort. Often, when opportunities present themselves, our instinct is to shy away, especially if they feel unfamiliar or daunting. But discomfort is a sign of growth. It's the universe's way of nudging you forward. There's an old saying: "When you're in the middle of a storm, God might send you a ship or a helicopter, but it's up to you to get on board." This time, I chose to step aboard.

Creating awareness and surrendering to what came my way— whether it was unexpected partnerships or challenging conversations—became the key to moving forward. Instead of resisting, I leaned in, trusting that each step would lead to something greater. Vincenzo, Nikita, and Pat weren't just part of my journey; they were catalysts for a new way of thinking and living, helping me embrace the positivity and possibility in front of me.

Takeaways: Reinvention

- **Embrace the Catalyst:** Rock bottom isn't the end—it's an opportunity for transformation. Use it to reassess and rebuild with clarity and purpose.
- **Pause with Intention:** Stopping isn't failure; it's creating space to reflect, heal, and recalibrate. Embrace stillness to rediscover your path.
- **Reconnect with Your Values:** Identify your core principles. When aligned with your actions, these values become the foundation of a purposeful life.
- **Lean Into Discomfort:** Growth lies outside your comfort zone. Don't shy away from the unfamiliar; embrace it as a catalyst for change.
- **Build Your Circle:** A strong support system is invaluable. Surround yourself with people who challenge, encourage, and hold you accountable.
- **Take Small, Consistent Steps:** Big changes come from small, deliberate actions. Celebrate progress and use it to build momentum.

Transformation is not about erasing the past; it's about embracing it as the foundation for a stronger future. When life breaks you open, it offers the opportunity to rebuild with clarity and intention, allowing you to align your actions with your core values and rediscovered purpose.

Every setback has the potential to be a setup for something greater. This journey isn't about merely bouncing back—it's about moving forward with wisdom, resilience, and a deeper connection to who you are. The lessons learned in your darkest moments can become the pillars of a life rebuilt on authenticity and strength.

The power to transform lies within you, waiting for the moment you choose to begin. By leaning into discomfort, surrounding yourself with a meaningful support system, and taking small yet purposeful steps, you create the momentum needed to write a new chapter— one that reflects your courage, growth, and unwavering belief in what's possible.

CHAPTER 13 - PART I:

THE RECALIBRATION BLUEPRINT
A PATH TO REINVENTION

Rock bottom wasn't my undoing—it was my rebirth. It was the moment life forced me to confront the truth: the way I had been living was unsustainable. After the financial collapse, the professional disappointments, and the personal unraveling, I had a choice—stay in the rubble or start rebuilding.

Recalibration isn't just about fixing what's broken; it's about rebuilding a life that aligns with your purpose. It's about creating a roadmap, step by step, to navigate out of the darkness and into a more authentic, fulfilling existence. For me, this journey was about shedding what no longer served me and embracing a new way of being. This recalibration guide is the result of that process.

Let's dive in.

Step One: Stop Everything (Pause to Heal)

When everything feels like it's spinning out of control, the first step is to stop. Not slow down. Not step back. Stop completely.

This was the hardest step for me. After declaring bankruptcy in January 2019, I tried to drink my way out of the pain, to drown the shame with parties, distractions, and anything that kept me from looking in the mirror. But that night in May 2019, sitting in that bathtub, I realized I couldn't run anymore. My only choice was to pause everything.

Stopping doesn't mean quitting; it means creating space. For me, it meant:

- **Eliminating toxic habits**: I stopped drinking entirely, not just for days but for months. Sobriety became the foundation of my clarity. One defining moment came after a particularly rough night out when I realized I was trying to escape my emotions instead of facing them. That realization became the turning point, pushing me to choose clarity over distraction.
- **Avoiding unhelpful environments**: I said no to nightlife, events, and social gatherings where I knew I couldn't be my best self. It was difficult at first, but each "no" felt like reclaiming a small piece of my autonomy.
- **Practicing radical stillness**: I spent hours sitting in silence, letting the emotions come without judgment. At first, it was excruciating to confront the chaos within, but one evening, during a quiet walk, I found a surprising sense of peace. That stillness became a liberating reminder that I didn't have to outrun my thoughts; I could simply let them be.

Stopping is an act of courage. It forces you to face the discomfort you've been avoiding. But it's also the only way to begin the healing process.

Step Two: Audit Your Life

Once the noise quiets, the next step is to take inventory—not just of your circumstances but of your strengths. When life knocks you down, it's easy to feel like you've lost everything. But the truth is, the skills, knowledge, and experiences you've gained over time remain. This audit isn't about what you've lost—it's about rediscovering what you still have and how to use it as a foundation for growth.

- **Skills and strengths**: Make a list of the abilities you've developed over the years. Are you a problem solver? A great communicator? These are assets that can guide your next steps. I recall sitting down one evening and realizing that my ability to connect people and build relationships was still intact—it became the cornerstone of my new path.

- **Relationships**: Evaluate the people in your life. Who uplifts you? Who drains you? Focus on strengthening connections with those who align with your values and vision. One pivotal moment for me was recognizing that certain relationships were no longer serving my growth, and I had to create space for new, supportive connections.
- **Positive habits**: Identify routines or behaviors that are already working for you. Maybe it's a morning walk or a weekly check-in with a mentor. Build on these small wins to create consistency and stability.

This audit isn't just about fixing what's broken; it's about recognizing your foundation and building upon it with intention.

Step Three: Rediscover Your Identity

Who are you when you strip away the labels, the titles, and the expectations? For years, I had identified myself as a restaurateur, an entrepreneur, a "success." But when those roles were taken away, I felt lost. This step was about rediscovering me.

I started by revisiting my roots:

- **Journaling**: Writing became my therapy. I explored my childhood, my motivations, and the moments that had shaped me. What lit me up? What had I always loved? One specific journal entry stands out: I described a memory from my early career, hosting an event where everyone felt connected and uplifted. That memory reminded me of my passion for creating spaces where people could thrive.
- **Reconnecting with my "why"**: I asked myself why I started my hospitality journey in the first place. The answer wasn't about money or recognition—it was about creating spaces where people felt seen and connected. Recalling this helped me reignite the sense of purpose I had lost.

- **Seeking feedback**: I had candid conversations with trusted friends and mentors, asking them how they saw me and what they believed my strengths were. One mentor shared, "Your ability to bring people together is your superpower." That insight became a cornerstone of how I redefined myself moving forward.

This process wasn't about finding a "new" identity; it was about uncovering the authentic self I had buried under layers of ambition and external validation.

Step Four: Build a Resilience Toolbox

Rebuilding isn't a straight line—it's a series of ups and downs. To navigate it, you need tools. This step was about equipping myself with practices and strategies that helped me stay grounded, focused, and resilient.

Here's what went into my toolbox:

- **Mindfulness and meditation**: I started meditating daily, even if it was just for five minutes. One particularly transformative session came after a stressful week when I managed to quiet my mind for the first time. That moment gave me a sense of calm I hadn't felt in years and reminded me of the power of presence.
- **Physical movement**: Walking became my therapy. It cleared my mind and gave me a sense of progress, one step at a time. I recall one evening walk where I found myself processing a difficult conversation from earlier in the day. By the time I returned home, I had clarity and a plan for how to address it.
- **Therapy and coaching**: Seeking professional help was a game changer. It provided me with insights and techniques to process emotions and develop healthier patterns. One session helped me reframe how I approached setbacks, turning them into learning opportunities.

- **Daily gratitude**: Every morning, I wrote down three things I was grateful for. One morning, after weeks of this practice, I found myself smiling at the simplicity of being grateful for clean air and sunshine. It shifted my perspective, reminding me of the beauty in everyday moments.

Your toolbox will look different from mine. The key is to find practices that resonate with you and commit to them consistently.

Step Five: Build Bridges to Progress

When you're rebuilding, the big picture can feel overwhelming. Instead of getting lost in long-term goals, I focused on creating bridges—steps that connected where I was to where I wanted to be. These bridges weren't flashy; they were deliberate, practical, and rooted in what I needed at the moment.

- **Financial clarity**: I started small by tracking every dollar I spent for a week. This simple act wasn't just about cutting costs but about understanding my habits and priorities. From there, I could redirect resources toward what truly mattered.
- **Physical renewal**: My first step was as small as committing to a five-minute stretch in the morning. Eventually, that grew into a consistent practice of movement that gave me energy and confidence.
- **Professional sparks**: Instead of diving into massive plans, I asked myself simple questions: What could I learn today? Who could I connect with? These small actions reignited my entrepreneurial spark without the pressure of an immediate outcome.

These bridges weren't just steps forward—they were reminders that progress isn't about leaps but about showing up consistently. By building these bridges, I created momentum that made the journey sustainable.

Step Six: Lean Into Your Community

Rebuilding isn't a solo journey. During this phase, I learned to lean on my support system in ways I never had before.

For me, this meant:

- **Reconnecting with family**: My wife became my anchor, reminding me of my worth even when I couldn't see it. Her unwavering support was a lifeline.
- **Seeking mentorship**: I reached out to former colleagues and mentors, asking for guidance and perspective. Their wisdom helped me see possibilities I hadn't considered.
- **Building new connections**: I started attending networking events and meeting people who inspired me. Surrounding myself with growth-oriented individuals was transformative.

Your community can be your greatest asset—if you let it.

Step Seven: Design Your Future

Once I had a stable foundation, it was time to dream again. But this time, I approached it differently. Instead of chasing external validation, I focused on creating a life that felt aligned.

Here's how I designed my future:

- **Visualization**: I imagined my ideal day in vivid detail—how I wanted to feel, who I wanted to be around, and what I wanted to create.
- **Reverse engineering**: I broke that vision into actionable steps, starting with what I could do today.
- **Staying flexible**: I allowed my vision to evolve as I grew, giving myself permission to pivot when needed.

Designing your future isn't about creating a rigid plan; it's about setting a direction and trusting the journey.

Expanded Takeaways

1. **Pause with Intention**: Stopping is an act of courage. Create space to reflect, heal, and recalibrate.
2. **Audit Your Life**: Get brutally honest about where you are. Awareness is the first step to change.
3. **Reconnect with Your Core**: Rediscover who you are beneath the roles and expectations.
4. **Equip Yourself**: Build a resilience toolbox with practices that ground and empower you.
5. **Celebrate Small Wins**: Focus on micro goals that create momentum and confidence.
6. **Lean on Your People**: Community is your safety net. Invest in relationships that uplift and challenge you.
7. **Dream Boldly**: Design a future that aligns with your values and passions.

Closing Remarks

This process wasn't easy, and it wasn't quick. Stopping everything and embracing stillness took months of discipline and courage. Auditing my life was humbling; confronting debts, toxic relationships, and unhealthy habits forced me to face truths I had long avoided. Rediscovering my identity wasn't an overnight revelation—it was a series of small realizations, built through journaling, conversations, and moments of clarity.

The entire recalibration process spanned years. The first few months were focused on stopping and creating stillness—detoxing from toxic habits and environments while sitting with the discomfort of reflection. Auditing my life and rediscovering my identity took the better part of a year, as I slowly peeled back layers of distraction and rediscovered my core values. Building a resilience toolbox and establishing habits like daily meditation and journaling required consistent effort over several more months, while setting and achieving micro-goals became a continual practice. There were days when I felt like I was moving backward, moments when doubt crept in, and times when it would have been easier to revert to old patterns. But I kept going because I realized that transformation is a lifelong commitment, not a quick fix.

My journey was unique to me, but the principles are universal. Wherever you are, know that it's never too late to pause, reflect, and recalibrate. Take the first step today—no matter how small—and trust that the path ahead will unfold as you continue to show up for yourself.

CHAPTER 13 - PART II

REBUILDING MOMENTUM
A JOURNEY THROUGH PILLARS AND PERSISTENCE

Momentum is the quiet force that turns effort into transformation. It doesn't come in flashes of brilliance or streaks of luck; it grows steadily through intentional actions. This chapter builds on the recalibration blueprint by showing how those foundational steps evolve into lasting habits fueled by the four key pillars: *Mindset, Heartset, Soulset, and Healthset.*

Your momentum is your story, and it's time to take the first step toward writing the next chapter of your life.

-

The First Push: Owning Your Vulnerability

Momentum starts with one honest, deliberate step. None of us want to admit we need help, but vulnerability is where transformation begins. My journey started when I enrolled in psychiatric therapy. Those sessions became the cornerstone for untangling the emotions and patterns I had ignored for far too long. Showing up in that room was my first act of self-commitment—a signal that I was ready to face the discomfort head-on.

After declaring bankruptcy in 2019, my life felt like quicksand. Drinking, isolation, and self-doubt had become my coping mechanisms. The first step to reclaiming myself wasn't about jumping into action but about stopping the cycle of avoidance and acknowledging where I was. Therapy helped me lay the groundwork for the changes that followed. It wasn't about grandeur or instant solutions—it was about showing up for myself with honesty and intention.

-

Mindset: Rewiring Your Inner Dialogue

Your thoughts shape your actions. Mastering your mindset is the first pillar of rebuilding momentum. It starts with rewiring the way you speak to yourself.

At my lowest, I felt trapped in a mental loop of failure. My thoughts were my greatest obstacle. Journaling became my lifeline. I began every morning with a stream of consciousness—pouring every frustration, fear, and regret onto paper. At first, it was chaotic. But over time, I began to notice patterns: self-blame, catastrophic thinking, and a constant comparison to the version of myself that had "succeeded."

I made a choice to challenge those thoughts. Instead of writing, *I've failed*, I asked, *What did I learn?* Instead of, *I can't recover from this*, I wrote, *What's one step forward today?*

- **Takeaway:** Start by identifying the patterns in your thoughts. Replace negative loops with questions that guide you toward growth. For example, during one journaling session, I noticed a recurring thought: "I've failed." I decided to challenge it by asking myself, "What did this failure teach me?" This reframing turned a moment of despair into an opportunity for reflection and growth, reinforcing the power of small mindset shifts.
- **Habit-Stacking Tip:** Pair your morning coffee with five minutes of journaling. Reflect on three things you're grateful for and one action you'll take to move forward.

Heartset: Reconnecting With Emotion and Compassion

Momentum isn't just a mental game—it's about emotional resilience and compassion for yourself and others.

During my downfall, I alienated myself from the people who mattered most. My wife, who had stood by me through every storm, was the first to say, "You're shutting me out." Those words stayed with me. I realized I couldn't rebuild momentum without connection.

One of the most healing moments came when I began openly sharing my fears and failures with her. That shift unlocked a deeper emotional resilience within me. It wasn't just about unburdening myself; it was about creating a safe space where vulnerability became a strength. These conversations helped me process emotions I had suppressed for years and built a sense of trust and connection that anchored me during challenging moments. This renewed bond gave me the momentum to face life's obstacles with a stronger, more compassionate heart.

- **Takeaway:** Don't isolate yourself. Connection isn't a luxury—it's a necessity. Lean into the relationships that anchor you, and don't be afraid to ask for help.
- **Habit-Stacking Tip:** Schedule time weekly for intentional connection—a date night, a walk with a close friend, or a call to someone who's supported you.

Soulset: Aligning With Purpose

True momentum isn't about doing more—it's about aligning with what matters. Rediscovering your "why" is the compass that guides your actions.

When I rebuilt, I asked myself one hard question: *Why am I here?* For years, my motivation had been tied to external validation—money, accolades, and proving I belonged. But those things didn't bring fulfillment. I sat with this question for weeks until clarity struck: I wanted to create, inspire, and connect.

I wrote down my non-negotiables: Family. Impact. Creativity. These became my North Star. Aligning decisions with these values transformed the way I approached each day. For example, when opportunities arose, I asked myself: "Does this align with my commitment to family? Will this create a meaningful impact?" This clarity simplified choices and ensured every step forward reflected my core purpose.

- **Takeaway:** Take the time to sit with your purpose. Strip away external expectations and focus on what truly drives you.
- **Habit-Stacking Tip:** Dedicate 10 minutes a day to purpose work. Reflect on how your daily actions align with your core values.

Healthset: Building Physical and Mental Resilience

Momentum requires energy, and energy comes from a healthy body and mind.

In the darkest days, my health hit rock bottom. I was drinking to numb the pain and ignoring my physical well-being. My wake-up call came during a doctor's visit when I realized I was on the edge of a serious health crisis.

I didn't overhaul my life overnight. Instead, I started small. A glass of water before my morning coffee. A 30-minute workout three times a week. Gradually, I began to feel stronger—mentally and physically. That strength carried into every other part of my life.

- **Takeaway:** Your physical and mental health are non-negotiable. Prioritize them, even in the busiest seasons of life.
- **Habit-Stacking Tip:** Build movement into your existing routines. For example, commit to a 10-minute walk after dinner or replace a late-night drink with a cup of herbal tea.

Momentum Through Habit-Stacking

The small steps you take in the beginning form the foundation for habit-stacking and building momentum. Each of these pillars builds on the others to create a sustainable system of growth. Mindset provides the mental clarity to navigate challenges, like identifying thought patterns through journaling as discussed earlier. Heartset fosters emotional resilience and connection, such as leaning into vulnerable conversations with loved ones to rebuild trust. Soulset aligns your actions with purpose, as seen in defining non-negotiables to guide decisions. Healthset fuels your physical and mental energy, starting with simple habits like drinking water or committing to movement.

These pillars aren't isolated—they interact dynamically. Journaling doesn't just clarify your mindset; it helps uncover emotional barriers tied to Heartset. Reconnecting with loved ones doesn't just strengthen relationships; it realigns actions with Soulset by fostering purpose. Every small action in one area creates a ripple effect, reinforcing progress across the others. By stacking habits and aligning them with your values, you create a sustainable framework for transformation.

Start with what you can control. You may not be able to rebuild your life overnight, but you can start with one habit that creates a positive shift.

Celebrate small wins. Progress isn't linear, but every step forward matters.

Be patient. Momentum isn't about speed—it's about consistency.

-

Takeaways: Creating a Blueprint for Momentum

1. **Start with Intentional Action**: Momentum begins with a single, deliberate choice. Choose one habit—journaling, a gratitude practice, or a 5-minute meditation—to ground yourself in positive change, aligning with your Mindset pillar.
2. **Build Consistency**: Success comes from showing up consistently, not from the size of your steps. Even on difficult days, focus on one action that aligns with your Healthset to maintain physical and mental resilience.
3. **Transform Setbacks into Learning**: View challenges as opportunities for growth. For example, use journaling to identify lessons from setbacks, reinforcing your Heartset through emotional resilience.
4. **Align with Your Core Values**: Use your values as a compass to guide decisions, as seen with Soulset—prioritize actions that align with purpose and what truly matters to you.
5. **Foster Meaningful Connections**: Invest in relationships that uplift and challenge you. Lean into Heartset by building a support system that anchors you during tough times and celebrates your progress.
6. **Prioritize Sustainability**: Focus on habits and routines that nourish you over the long term, linking directly to your Healthset. Small, consistent steps create lasting transformation and momentum.

CHAPTER 14: OWN YOUR NEXT CHAPTER

On January 21, 2019, I hit rock bottom. Declaring bankruptcy wasn't just a financial collapse; it was a moment that stripped away every illusion of control I thought I had. It was raw, humiliating, and terrifying. I had poured my soul into building something I thought defined me, only to watch it disintegrate. But here's the truth: rock bottom wasn't the end—it was the fucking reset button I didn't know I needed. It was the moment I stopped running, stopped pretending, and started rebuilding from the ground up.

Transformation doesn't come wrapped in a bow or handed to you in some neatly packaged epiphany. It's gritty, messy, and fucking relentless. It demands everything you've got—and then some. Over the last five years, I turned over every fucking rock to untangle my mind and rebuild my soul. I sat with Ayahuasca. I faced my fears with Bufo and Kambo. I explored the depths of my consciousness with Joe Dispenza's meditations and Tony Robbins' seminars. Each modality cracked me open in ways I didn't know were possible. This chapter isn't a neat ending; it's your rally cry. It's the moment you grab the pen and decide to write your own damn story, unapologetically and with everything you've got. But it's also the most liberating, soul-shaking thing you'll ever do.

Reflecting on the Journey

Take a hard look at where you are right now. Maybe you're standing in the wreckage of something you thought would last forever. Maybe you're at a crossroads, stuck between fear and the unknown. Wherever you are, know this: you are not alone, and you are not fucking done. This isn't about creating some perfect version of yourself—it's about owning your shit, building momentum, and living this one life with ferocity and purpose.

You've learned that recalibration begins with pause. It's about stopping, reflecting, and reassessing the foundations you've built your life upon. You've explored the importance of small, intentional steps to rebuild, whether through reconnecting with your identity, embracing vulnerability, or finding strength in a support system. You've learned how breaking old patterns through radical modalities can crack open truths you've buried for years and bring clarity to the path ahead. And you've discovered how the four pillars—Mindset, Heartset, Soulset, and Healthset—interact to create a sustainable framework for growth.

The Power of Choice

The most transformative lesson I've learned is that your life is defined by the choices you make. Every decision I made—to walk into that therapist's office, to face my fears through plant medicine, to sit in the discomfort of my own mind—was a brick in the foundation of the man I've become. I chose to prioritize healing over hiding, alignment over approval. I built a life rooted in my core values: Family. Impact. Creativity.

You have that same power. Every moment, you have the opportunity to choose. To choose purpose over distraction. Connection over isolation. Progress over perfection. These choices are not always easy, but they are always yours.

Your Next Five Years

If there's one thing, I hope you take from this book, it's this: Transformation is possible. No matter where you are today, you are not defined by your setbacks. You are defined by how you respond to them.

Picture yourself five years from now. What does your life look like? Are you still spinning your wheels in the same cycles, or have you broken free? Who have you become? What have you created? The future isn't waiting for you—it's built by the choices you make today. Get clear. Get raw. Decide what matters most, and take the first fucking step. Not tomorrow, not when you're ready—right now.

A Note of Gratitude

This book isn't just my story—it's a conversation between the raw, broken parts of me and the parts of you that are still fighting to rise. Writing this has been one of the hardest, most humbling experiences of my life. But it's also been a fucking privilege—to stand here, five years after bankruptcy, as a testament to what's possible when you refuse to quit. To those who believed in me, to those who doubted me, to those who walked this path before me— thank you. And to the badass version of you that's just waiting to rise—thank you for showing the fuck up. Let's go.

Call to Action

This book is just the beginning. Your beginning. Whether it's journaling through the chaos, calling a therapist, or choosing to stop running from yourself, your next chapter starts now. Don't wait for permission. Don't wait for perfect conditions. Just start. And when you do? Share your fucking story. Show the world what's possible when you decide to live life on your own terms. The pen is in your hand. Write something fucking incredible.

STAY CONNECTED WITH GAURAV 'G' PATEL

Thank you for joining me on this journey. Your engagement means the world to me, and I'd love to keep the conversation going. Below are the ways you can connect with me, learn more about my work, and stay updated on future projects.

-

WEBSITE

Visit my website for updates, exclusive content, and insights: http://www.gpatel.co

-

NEWSLETTER

Sign up for my newsletter to receive updates about upcoming projects, personal insights, and exclusive offers: https://gpreneur.beehiiv.com/

-

SOCIAL MEDIA

Let's connect on social media! Follow me for regular updates, behind-the-scenes content, and direct interaction:

- Instagram:
  - Author: https://www.instagram.com/gpatel.co/
  - Personal: https://www.instagram.com/gpatel.me/

- LinkedIn: https://www.linkedin.com/in/gpreneur
- X - Twitter: https://x.com/NothnButAGThing

FOR SPEAKING ENGAGEMENTS

Interested in having me speak at your event? Let's make it happen.
Visit: http://www.gpatel.co

-

EVENTS AND WEBINARS

Stay tuned for upcoming virtual events, live Q&A sessions, and workshops. Keep an eye on my website or social media for announcements!

-

CONTACT ME

I value your feedback and would love to hear from you!

Email: author@gpatel.co
Mailing Address: PO Box 626, Raleigh, NC 27602

-

Thank you for reading and for being a part of this journey. Together, we're creating stories that inspire, challenge, and transform. I look forward to connecting with you and hearing your thoughts.

INDEX: TAKEAWAYS

- **Reconnect with Your Core Values**
  What principles guide your decisions? Family? Integrity? Hard work? Write them down, and commit to living by them.

- **Create Rituals That Ground You**
  Whether it's a daily walk, a quiet moment of reflection, or a bowl of yogurt, find small practices that keep you connected to what matters most.

- **Lean on Your Community**
  Nobody succeeds alone, succeeding alone is an oxymoron. Surround yourself with people who uplift and challenge you, and don't be afraid to lean on them when the road gets tough.

- **Language Is Power**
  Learning the language of your environment—whether it's a literal language or the unspoken rules of a new culture—is the first step to integration.

- **Reinvent Without Losing Yourself**
  Adapting doesn't mean abandoning who you are. It means building bridges between your past and your present.

- **Resilience Is Built, Not Born**
  Each challenge, each failure, each misstep is an opportunity to grow stronger. Adaptation isn't a one-time thing; it's a lifelong process.

- **Community Matters**
  Surround yourself with people who believe in you, who guide you, and who remind you of what's possible.

- *Bet on Yourself*
  Taking risks is scary, but the rewards can be life-changing. Trust yourself enough to take the leap.

- **Hustle Is About Consistency**
  Success isn't about one big move—it's about showing up every day, putting in the work, and staying consistent.

- **Relationships Are Everything**
  The connections I made through my events weren't just transactional—they were transformational. Always invest in people.

- **Adapt and Evolve**
  Nothing ever goes perfectly, but every challenge is an opportunity to learn, grow, and adapt.

- **Question Everything**
  Rules aren't sacred. Challenge them, test them, and figure out which ones serve you and which ones hold you back.

- **Find Your Hustle**
  Whether it's selling candy bars or starting a business, find something that's yours. It's not about the money—it's about the independence and confidence it gives you.

- **Embrace Your Differences**
  Stop trying to fit in. Your differences are your strengths, the things that set you apart and make you valuable.

- **Build on Your Foundations**
  Remember where you came from, but don't let it limit you. Use it as a springboard to reach higher.

- *Bet on Yourself*
  Taking risks is scary, but the rewards can be life-changing. Trust yourself enough to take the leap.

- *Hustle Is About Consistency*
  Success isn't about one big move—it's about showing up every day, putting in the work, and staying consistent.

- *Relationships Are Everything*
  The connections I made through my events weren't just transactional—they were transformational. Always invest in people.

- *Adapt and Evolve*
  Nothing ever goes perfectly, but every challenge is an opportunity to learn, grow, and adapt.

- *Mistakes Are Catalysts, Not Endings*
  What feels like failure in the moment is often just a lesson in disguise. Every fall is an opportunity to rise stronger.

- *Trust but Verify*
  Ambition is important, but so is caution. Always do your homework, ask the hard questions, and trust your instincts.

- *The Importance of a Support System*
  My father and Sachin didn't abandon me when I stumbled. They reminded me that resilience isn't a solo act—it's built on the shoulders of those who believe in you.

- *Keep Moving*
  The only way out of a setback is through it. Learn, adapt, and keep moving forward.

- *Keep the Door Open*
  Relationships are currency. Stay connected, even when things go wrong. You never know which bridge will lead to your next opportunity.

- *Plan With Precision*
  Big dreams require sharp execution. Do your homework,

double-check everything, and leave nothing to chance.

- **Celebrate the Comeback**
  Success isn't just about the peaks—it's about how you climb out of the valleys. Celebrate the journey as much as the destination.

- **Resilience Is a Muscle**
  The more you use it, the stronger it gets. Every setback is an opportunity to grow.

- **Build with Purpose**
  Every concept needs a clear vision. Customers don't just want products; they want experiences.

- **Invest in People**
  Your employees are your greatest asset. Empower them, support them, and they'll drive your vision forward.

- **Pivot, Always**
  Hospitality requires adaptability. Whether it's shifting a concept or revamping operations, staying rigid is a recipe for failure.

- **Know Your Market**
  Data is a powerful tool. Understanding customer behavior and market trends allowed us to stay ahead.

- **Create Community**
  Success isn't just about profits—it's about impact. Building relationships with customers, employees, and the community creates a foundation that lasts.

- **Embrace Humility**
  Growth is exciting, but unchecked ambition can lead to overextension. Learn to recognize your limits and adjust

before the cracks widen.

- **Focus on Sustainability**
  It's not just about scaling up; it's about ensuring that growth is manageable and sustainable. Sometimes, less is more.

- **Listen to Your Team**
  As a leader, it's easy to get caught up in your vision. But your team's feedback is invaluable. They're in the trenches and often see problems before you do.

- **Prioritize Relationships**
  Success is meaningless if it comes at the cost of your relationships. Make time for the people who matter, even in the midst of chaos.

- **Adapt and Rebuild**
  Challenges are inevitable, but how you respond defines your path forward. Don't be afraid to pivot, let go of failing ventures, and focus on what's truly important.

- **Grow Strategically, Not Recklessly**
  Expansion is exciting, but it can also be your downfall. Focus on sustainable growth, ensuring you have the infrastructure and cash flow to support it.

- **Build a Financial Safety Net**
  In a volatile industry, reserves are your lifeline. Plan for the unexpected because the unexpected will come.

- **Separate Your Identity from Your Business**
  It's easy to tie your self-worth to your success, but your value is not determined by P&L statements.

- **Embrace Failure as a Catalyst**
  Setbacks are not the end—they're opportunities to learn, pivot, and come back stronger.

- *Prioritize Your Health and Relationships*
  No business is worth sacrificing your well-being or the people you love. Make time for self-care and nurture your personal connections.

- *Be Transparent with Your Team*
  Your employees are your greatest asset. Keep them informed, involve them in problem-solving, and show them you value their contributions.

- *Embrace the Catalyst*
  Rock bottom isn't the end—it's an opportunity for transformation. Use it to reassess and rebuild with clarity and purpose.

- *Pause with Intention*
  Stopping isn't failure; it's creating space to reflect, heal, and recalibrate. Embrace stillness to rediscover your path.

- *Reconnect with Your Values*
  Identify your core principles. When aligned with your actions, these values become the foundation of a purposeful life.

- *Lean Into Discomfort*
  Growth lies outside your comfort zone. Don't shy away from the unfamiliar; embrace it as a catalyst for change.

- *Build Your Circle*
  A strong support system is invaluable. Surround yourself with people who challenge, encourage, and hold you accountable.

- *Take Small, Consistent Steps*
  Big changes come from small, deliberate actions. Celebrate progress and use it to build momentum.

- *Pause with Intention*
  Stopping is an act of courage. Create space to reflect, heal,

and recalibrate.

- **Audit Your Life**
  Get brutally honest about where you are. Awareness is the first step to change.

- **Reconnect with Your Core**
  Rediscover who you are beneath the roles and expectations.

- **Equip Yourself**
  Build a resilience toolbox with practices that ground and empower you.

- **Celebrate Small Wins**
  Focus on micro goals that create momentum and confidence.

- **Lean on Your People**
  Community is your safety net. Invest in relationships that uplift and challenge you.

- **Dream Boldly**
  Design a future that aligns with your values and passions.

- **Start with Intentional Action**
  Momentum begins with a single, deliberate choice. Choose one habit—journaling, a gratitude practice, or a 5-minute meditation—to ground yourself in positive change, aligning with your Mindset pillar.

- **Build Consistency**
  Success comes from showing up consistently, not from the size of your steps. Even on difficult days, focus on one action that aligns with your Healthset to maintain physical and mental resilience.

- *Transform Setbacks into Learning*
  View challenges as opportunities for growth. For example, use journaling to identify lessons from setbacks, reinforcing your Heartset through emotional resilience.

- *Align with Your Core Values*
  Use your values as a compass to guide decisions, as seen with Soulset—prioritize actions that align with purpose and what truly matters to you.

- *Foster Meaningful Connections*
  Invest in relationships that uplift and challenge you. Lean into Heartset by building a support system that anchors you during tough times and celebrates your progress.

- *Prioritize Sustainability*
  Focus on habits and routines that nourish you over the long term, linking directly to your Healthset. Small, consistent steps create lasting transformation and momentum.

TOP 50 QUOTES BY G. PATEL

1. "Rock bottom isn't the end—it's your restart."

2. "Success isn't about avoiding failure—it's about learning how to rebuild."

3. "Resilience isn't bouncing back—it's crawling forward when you can't stand."

4. "Growth starts where comfort ends."

5. "Each challenge is a steppingstone to the person you're meant to become."

6. "Life's greatest lessons often come wrapped in adversity."

7. "Adaptation isn't a compromise; it's a strength."

8. "You can't rebuild without first letting go of what's broken."

9. "Celebrate progress, no matter how small."

10. "Your foundation isn't perfect—it's what holds you steady when life shakes."

11. "Mindset is your superpower; guard it fiercely."

12. "The spiral stops when you decide to climb out."

13. "Perspective turns failures into opportunities."

14. "Belief systems are like a compass—they guide every step."

15. "Don't chase perfection; pursue progress."

16. "Your limitations are only as real as you believe them to be."

17. "Focus on what you can control and let go of the rest."

18. "Challenges don't define you; how you respond to them does."

19. "Every experience shapes the lens through which you see the world."

20. "Where your attention goes, your energy flows."

21. "Sometimes, all it takes is one person believing in you to create momentum."

22. "You are your own lifeline—no one is coming to save you."

23. "Every setback carries the seed of a comeback."

24. "Motivation fades; discipline builds success."

25. "Start messy; perfection will never arrive on day one."

26. "Find your reason, and you'll find your way."

27. "Your dreams don't work unless you do."

28. "Turn 'what if' into 'why not?'"

29. "Small actions compound into massive results."

30. "Every big achievement starts with a single, uncertain step."

31. "The darkest moments teach you to shine the brightest."

32. "Life is a series of unexpected outcomes; embrace the ride."

33. "Success without purpose is empty."

34. "Balance is not a destination but a way of being."

35. "Be a chameleon—adapt and thrive."

36. "Hustle without heart is just noise."

37. "The stories we tell ourselves shape the lives we live."

38. "Gratitude turns what we have into enough."

39. "Your past informs you, but it doesn't define you."

40. "Community is your safety net; cherish it."

41. "Savor the journey—don't just build, live."

42. "When you face the unknown, lean into curiosity."

43. "Rebuilding starts with owning your truth."

44. "Turn rebellion into purpose, and you'll change the game."

45. "Respect the hands that labor—it's a lesson in humility."

46. "The unknown isn't something to fear; it's where growth lives."

47. "Embrace the duality—roots in one world, wings in another."

48. "Anchor yourself with rituals that keep you grounded."

49. "Faith in the journey matters more than the certainty of the destination."

50. "Rewrite your story—no one else has the pen."

72731202R00065